The Incarnate Christ

The Incarnate Christ

An Engineer's Quest to Define
the Person of Christ

Robert Von Schriltz

VANTAGE PRESS
New York

Unless otherwise specified, all Bible quotations are from the New American Standard Bible, copyright 1960, 1962, 1963, 1968, 1971, 1972, 1973, 1975, 1977, The Lockman Foundation, La Habra, California. Quoted scripture marked "NIV" is taken from the Holy Bible, New International Version, copyright 1973, 1978, 1984 by International Bible Society. Used by permission of Zondervan Publishing House.

FIRST EDITION

All rights reserved, including the right of reproduction in whole or in part in any form.

Copyright © 2003 by Robert Von Schriltz

Published by Vantage Press, Inc.
516 West 34th Street, New York, New York 10001

Manufactured in the United States of America
ISBN: 0-533-14434-5

Library of Congress Catalog Card No.: 2002094294

0 9 8 7 6 5 4 3 2 1

Now this is eternal life: that they may know you, the only true God, and Jesus Christ, whom you have sent (John 17:3, NIV).

Contents

Figures ix
Preface xi

   I. Purpose and Method   1
  II. The Trinity   9
 III. The Person of Christ   67

Appendix: Comparison Table   117

Figures

1. The "Manufacturing Process" of the Proposed Theological System — 5
2. Realm Information — 13
3. The Ontological Order — 41
4. The Progression of Prophecy — 45
5. The Progression of Prayer — 46
6. The Omnipresence of the Trinity Before Christ's Incarnation and After His Resurrection — 50
7. The Incarnate Christ's Likeness to Man — 81
8. The Omnipresence of the Trinity During the Earthly Years of the Incarnate Christ — 83

Preface

Jesus of Nazareth was Immanuel, God with us. This staggering reality has challenged creative thinkers for nearly two thousand years. Few have wrestled with this mystery quite like the theologians of the fourth century. Within the context of Greek thought, they spent a great deal of time debating the person of Christ, i.e., who he is in and of himself. While rejecting such views as Docetism, Ebonism, Arianism, Nestorianism, Eutychianism, and Appolinarianism, leading theologians developed the orthodox definition: Christ is a single person with two natures, one human and the other divine, and a physical body (of flesh and bones). I appreciate the great effort of the early church theologians. They made a noble attempt to find the real Jesus of the Bible. However, I must admit, the fourth-century Christological solution sounds somewhat foreign to my twenty-first-century ears.

Given the biblical evidence and the context in which it was written, how would you define the person of Christ? Would your solution look much like the early church theologians'? The following investigation is my answer to this formidable question, my quest to define the person of Christ in a personally relevant and meaningful way. As a means to this end, I will define him in this study using methods, ideas, and terminology that fit my world-view, my current life situation. This does not mean that I do not agree with the orthodox solution in some fundamental ways. For example, I believe in a trinity of Father, Son, and Holy Spirit. I also agree that the incarnate Christ is an eternal being, unique as the Son of God. Nevertheless, our agreement on the surface is not without significant difference at a deeper level, difference rooted in very different approaches to theology.

My background includes a degree in Industrial and Systems Engineering as well as work experience in several engineering environments. As an engineer, I learned to approach any given task in a certain way. An engineer is a problem-solver and innovator, always striving to do the job in a more effective and efficient manner. An engineer will experiment with new ideas and implement them if such change will improve the overall situation. This "engineering approach" typifies how I address problems in general, and, more relevant here, how I addressed the theological challenge at hand. Of course, this approach requires one to be as objective as possible. In this study, I did not take anything for granted or just assume something was right, regardless of who said it or how long it has been said (except, of course, for sacred Scripture itself). While the past is important and taken seriously, and at every step of theological development I sought to learn from those before me, I did not feel bound to affirm, defend, or deny earlier efforts. System integrity and coherence took precedence over creeds and tradition.

This pioneering spirit will be evident throughout this investigation as I outline an alternative—and hopefully more equitable—solution. I must also point out that the trail I will cut will not be entirely new. The proposed theory is similar in some respects to the Word-flesh Christologies of theologians such as Athanasius and Apollinarius; and because they are similar, it is only natural that they raise similar concerns. Therefore, some questions asked in the past must be asked again. The objections lodged against the Word-flesh Christologies of the early church presented a formidable challenge. On the one hand, I felt obligated to address all such criticism. On the other hand, I was hesitant to do so. The Christological debate of the early church presupposed a unique philosophical world-view, which greatly colored their Christological statements. This unique environment—an environment immersed in Greek thought—provided the setting for theological dialogue and thus helped to shape the types of questions that were raised by the opposition. Apart from this world-view, it is debatable which objections remain meaningful and valid. For this reason, I will not address all the objections lodged against early Word-flesh Christologies. Considerable attention will be given to several notable points of concern, the nature of Christ's humanity and his limitations.

This study will take a systematic approach to Christology. It will attempt to integrate a large amount of biblical information to form a single, cohesive system. This approach presents some perplexing challenges, which must be addressed with logic and creative imagination; and unavoidably, it provides a solution with a certain amount of theoretical speculation. All things considered, however, I do not believe that the approach adopted in this study is incompatible with a historical approach to Christology, or that the incarnate Christ put forth is at odds with the "historical" Jesus.

For the last several years, there has been a search under way within the academic community to find the historical Jesus, i.e., the Jesus who best fits into and is in harmony with the context of first-century Judaism. To date, this search has revealed many valuable insights about Jesus and his mission. But a purely historical approach does have its shortcomings and raises some questions of its own. Even after subjecting the New Testament text to the most critical historical analysis, there still remains the unshakable impression that the biblical writers considered Jesus to be something more than a spirit-filled man, a prophet, a sage . . . something more than a man par excellence. While the historical perspective is essential to understanding the person of Christ, it is restrictive and cannot, in and of itself, fully define him. It is my hope that the proposed solution will provide this "something more" and serve to complement historical research, with both together giving a fuller picture of Jesus of Nazareth, the Son of God.

My view of Scripture and its relationship to Christology is straightforward. I do not presume that the Gospels are narratives that are inappropriate for theological development, while the Epistles are the true building blocks of theology. Neither do I embrace an ever-evolving Christology, in which a primitive Christology in the early writings mutated into more sophisticated Christologies in the later writings. Lastly, I do not apply critical methodology to the text to determine who borrowed what from whom in order to find what was the original—and perhaps the more correct— wording. Instead, I believe the original autographs were inspired by God, accurate and truthful in all they contain; and that the copies we possess maintain the integrity of the originals. I treat all New Testament writings with equal value and authority. Each New Testament writer's unique personality and vocabulary as well as the particular circumstances and audience addressed account for the diverse descriptions of Jesus found in the pages of the New Testament. Though they vary in content and emphasis, each New Testament writing has a common subject: Jesus Christ. This commonality is, for example, what ties together the Christology of Mark with that of Paul. And, in this study, this commonality was my justification for freely yet thoughtfully placing a Christological idea of one writer alongside that of another. All the New Testament writers sought to put into words what they knew to be true about the same person, and ultimately their individual descriptions find harmony in him.

Like the early church theologians, my particular world-view colors the methods and conclusion of this investigation. While I may have eliminated some difficulties associated with the early Word-flesh Christologies, I may have also introduced new challenges foreign to the fourth-century Christological debate. Unfortunately, the difficult task at hand requires one to make assumptions, and the theologian must make these assumptions without sacrificing what he or she believes to be truly important or essential. The process may involve affirming one thing while sacrificing another. The pursuit of new ideas, especially in sacred things, is risky business. But one must often take such risks to grow both intellectually and spiritually. In time, I am sure that some of my current beliefs will change and thus render some of what is presented here obsolete. This investigation offers my thoughts at a particular point in time, a snapshot of an ongoing process and lifelong pursuit. I reserve the right to change with the introduction of new input. Nonetheless, this quest has thus far been a truly rewarding experience. It is my hope that like-minded pioneers who share in the following adventure find it to be a rewarding experience as well.

Unless otherwise noted, all biblical quotes are taken from the *New American Standard Version*. I also employ a variety of quotes and ideas from past as well as present Christian thinkers. When borrowing such things from others, I utilized endnotes to give credit where credit is due; however, such borrowing does not imply that the originator would agree, in part or in whole, with the theological system presented in this study. Finally, I have attempted to avoid sexist language. But this objective was much more difficult than I imagined. For example, I utilized the phrases *inner-man* and *outer-man* vice *inner-person* and *outer-person*. Due to the confusion associated with the word *person,* I thought it best to retain the traditional wording. I apologize beforehand for language that displays my lack of sensitivity.

The Incarnate Christ

I. Purpose and Method

At times, I feel that I know Jesus. He was raised in a rural suburb, experienced a normal upbringing, learned a common trade, paid his share of taxes, and attended religious services on weekends. He grew in wisdom, wept on occasion, suffered fatigue from overwork, struggled in prayer, and was willing to admit that he did not know something. He was angered by injustice and amazed at great faith. He confronted religious hypocrites with the truth, showed kindness to those down on their luck, made time for children, and invited everyone to the party. He was a good listener, both accessible and trustworthy. He was an honest person, the perfect neighbor, and a true friend.

    This Jesus is of the unsung, workaday hero variety. I know this Jesus because I know others like him. But the biblical writers will not let me hold on to this simple image too long. It slips through my hands like a wet bar of soap. The familiar is often eclipsed by the unfamiliar. The biblical writers said extraordinary things about Jesus. He turned water into wine, walked on the sea, stilled a storm, and fed thousands with a single lunch. He overpowered demonic forces, cleansed lepers, restored sight to the blind and hearing to the deaf, and raised the dead. He knew what people were thinking and spoke of the future as if it were yesterday's news. This Jesus is unlike anyone I know. He is unusual. He is startling. He is disturbing.

    Jesus is both typical and atypical, common and uncommon. He is a lot like us, yet he is not like anyone. Perhaps the word that best describes him is *unique*. The biblical writers knew that Jesus was a unique person. Yes, they described him as a vulnerable man who lived among common folk. But they also described him as God's only begotten Son. He was called the radiance of God's "glory and the exact representation of His nature" (Heb. 1:3). In Christ "all the fullness of Deity dwells in bodily form" (Col. 2:9). A simple carpenter, proclaimed "the image of the invisible God, the first-born of all creation" (1:15).

Who is this Jesus? How was he both natural and supernatural, both human and divine? How could he be born in time, yet exist before the creation of the world? How could he suffer fatigue, yet have the power to control nature? How could he lack knowledge, yet appear to know all things? How could he grow in wisdom, yet embody the wisdom of God? This study will develop a one-nature theory of the person of Christ and address such mysteries.

A. Building a Theological System

The 1991 *Random House Webster's College Dictionary* defines a system as "an assemblage or combination of things or parts forming a complex or unitary whole." Similarly, a *theological system* may be thought of as an assemblage of biblical truths forming a cohesive statement that defines a specific area of theology. This study will develop just such a system. In general, it will develop a theological system relating to the area of Christology. In particular, it will develop a system that defines the person of Christ. In preparation for tackling this objective, let's first discuss how to build and evaluate a theological system. The following illustration will prove helpful.

My father was a machinist by trade. He owned and operated a small machine shop, which built printing machines, machines designed to print logos and other relevant information on corrugated packing boxes. He would often take me to work with him to learn the family business. We would work side by side fabricating and assembling printers. He taught me how to work with my hands, think on my feet, and persevere until the job was complete.

A printing machine is manufactured in several stages. The first stage is chassis fabrication. Chassis fabrication begins with raw materials. We cut metal plates to size and welded them together to form a box-shaped structure—the chassis proper. Its dimensions are about eight feet long, four feet wide, and four feet high. Next, we drilled holes in the chassis and secured brackets to it to support an assortment of components. Finally, we painted the chassis to prevent corrosion. Throughout this process, care must be taken to construct the chassis according to design specifications. A misplaced hole or crooked bracket that goes undetected during the fabrication stage may prove disastrous. In one case, we completely disassembled a malfunctioning printer in order to locate the problem; and, as it turned out, the problem was a flaw in the chassis. To minimize the possibility of such problems down the road, it is best to thoroughly examine the chassis before proceeding to the next stage of manufacturing.

The next stage of manufacturing is unit assembly. We assembled the necessary components onto the chassis to complete the unit. We bolted the primary motor to a bracket located on the lower plate. Then we fastened the appropriate bearings to opposing sides of the chassis. These bearings are used to support several types of rollers, i.e., a metal cylinder with tapered ends, which looks much like an oversized rolling pin. The preeminent roller is referred to as the large drum roller. Attached to this roller is a rubber template, which, when covered in ink and rolled over the surface of the cardboard, prints the appropriate logo or wording on the cardboard. The assembly process moved forward. Gears, belts, electrical boxes and wiring, the ink reservoir, safety guards, and so forth, each component was methodically fastened, installed, or secured in place. Once complete, the printer was ready for testing.

The way we tested a printing machine was to evaluate the product it produced. In general, the quality of the product was used to determine the quality of the unit. After filling the ink reservoir and securing a template on the drum roller, we turned on the machine and fed through a piece of cardboard. If it consistently printed a quality pattern, the printer was ready for shipment to the customer. However, if it did not print a quality pattern, minor adjustments were made to, for example, roller height or motor speed to correct the problem. If the problem could not be rectified by making minor adjustments, an extensive examination was conducted to isolate the problem and make the necessary repairs.

This manufacturing process served as the pattern for figure 1. It graphically illustrates the "process," which will be used to build and test the proposed theological system. The first stage of the theological "manufacturing process" is "chassis fabrication," where "raw materials" are "fabricated" into a trinitarian "chassis." This will be accomplished by extracting from Scripture relevant passages concerning the Father, the Son, and the Holy

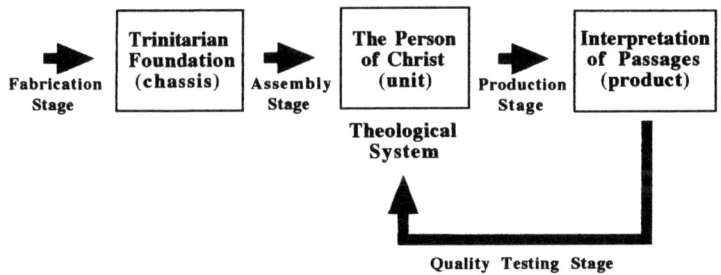

Figure 1: The "Manufacturing Process" of the Proposed Theological System

Spirit. This information will be used to develop a trinitarian concept that describes the relationship the persons of the trinity have with one another and with creation. The fabrication stage will be discussed in chapter 2.

The second stage of the theological "manufacturing process" is "unit assembly." Upon the trinitarian foundation, a theory of the person of Christ will be "assembled" together, using an assortment of "components" culled from the biblical text. These "components" include passages that say something pertinent about the person of Christ. The goal of the assembly stage is to produce a complete "unit," or theological system, which will pass "quality inspection." The assembly stage will be discussed in chapter 3.

The third stage of the theological "manufacturing process" is "product production." Here, the complete "unit" will produce a "product." The theological system—or the theory of the person of Christ established upon the trinitarian foundation—will be used to interpret selected passages relating to the incarnate Christ's knowledge. How well it interprets these passages as well as any associated issues that surface concerning the logical coherence of the system will provide a basis for determining the "quality" of the theological system. The production stage will be discussed towards the end of chapter 3.

The final stage of the theological "manufacturing process" is "quality testing." The "product" will be evaluated to determine the "quality" of the "unit." This is where the skill of the inspector comes into play, to look in the right places and ask the right questions. Does the system aid in our understanding of the passage? Or, does it severely alter or even deny the clear meaning intended by the author? While addressing the passages, does an inherent flaw in the system rise to the surface, i.e., something that proves to have no apparent or simple solution? In my closing comments, I will address such questions and use them as a yardstick to measure the "quality" of the proposed system, to determine if it is a credible and sound theory of the incarnate Christ.

B. Challenge to the Reader

Throughout my Bible college and seminary years, I was taught doctrine grounded in the historic Christian faith. During this time I learned about the major theological players, both past and present, as well as what they believed. I was also introduced to many theological books and articles, which added a great deal of depth to my learning experience. For this study, my background proved to be invaluable as I wrestled with the issues in search of a new path. While I will sometimes discuss "orthodox" doctrine concerning the trinity and the person of Christ as I present my argument, I will only scratch the surface of things.[1] Those unfamiliar with this subject matter would benefit greatly by doing some additional research outside this study.[2] The better one understands the orthodox position, the more equipped one will be to assess the value of what is being proposed.

The reader must bear in mind that the *purpose* of this investigation is not to affirm, defend, or deny orthodox doctrine.[3] This study is a personal quest, a quest to develop a *better* theory of the person of Christ, which is biblical, logical, and personally relevant. To develop something new often requires one to walk off the beaten path, over hills and through valleys seldom traveled and enjoyed. Sometimes when doing so, it is necessary to clear brush and chop limbs to make forward progress. It is hard work, which strains the back and makes the hands calloused. But the journey is worth the effort. The struggle makes one strong, and the sights along the way are precious and memorable. This word-picture accurately portrays the nature of this quest. In retrospect, it was a struggle every step of the way, yet it built my faith, providing me with insight and understanding I could not have gained any other way.

Theology involves the study of sacred things. Therefore, one must have a respect and healthy fear of the Lord when discussing his person and ways. After all, theology is not talking about a God who used to be, but a God who is living and active in his creation, a God who can be honored or insulted, pleased or disappointed. This investigation was conducted with the utmost care. However, no theology is perfect. The theological system presented in this study will not prove to be an exception. I encourage the reader to approach this work with a healthy skepticism. "Examine everything carefully; hold fast to that which is good" (1 Thess. 5:21).

Notes

1. Orthodox doctrine of the trinity and the person of Christ is rooted in two early creeds, namely, the Nicene Creed and the Chalcedonian Creed.
2. Several recommended works are J. Pelikan's five-volume *The Christian Tradition* (Chicago: The University of Chicago Press, 1971–1989), which gives a comprehensive history of doctrine and T. Oden's three-volume *Systematic Theology* (New York: Harper Collins, 1987–1992), which expresses the consensus view of Christian theology.
3. This purpose does not mean that the final *product* will necessarily disagree with all creeds. In fact, I contend that the proposed solution is compatible with the Apostle's Creed, a very early and universally accepted statement of faith.

II. The Trinity

Moses proclaimed to the people: "To you it was shown that you might know that the Lord, He is God; there is no other besides Him" (Deut. 4:35). These words summarize the Old Testament witness of God: the God of heaven and earth, the God of Israel is the only true and living God. This rich monotheistic heritage was alive and well in the first century. The New Testament writers unanimously affirmed the God of Abraham, Isaac, and Jacob. However, in the process of doing so, they also unveiled something more—a trinitarian revelation of God the Father, his unique Son, and a personal Spirit. While providing clarity this new revelation raises some difficult and perplexing questions. What can be affirmed about each person of this tri-unity? How do they relate to one another? How do they relate to creation? How can the trinity of the Father, the Son, and the Holy Spirit be reconciled with Old Testament monotheism? The goal of this chapter is to develop a concept of the trinity that will address such questions and serve as the foundation of the proposed theological system.

A. Defining Key Words and Concepts

Before discussing the persons of the trinity and the trinity proper, several key words and concepts require special attention. The word *person* will be used extensively throughout this investigation. Because this word has a wide variety of meanings, its use can be problematic. In the first century it meant *mask*. It was often used to describe the role of an actor in a play. Over the years it took on additional meanings. *Random House Webster's College Dictionary* lists eight uses for the word "person": (1) a human being; a man, woman, or child, (2) a human being as distinguished from an animal or a thing, (3) the actual self or individual personality of a human being, (4) the body of a living human being, (5) the body in its external aspects, (6) a human being or other entity, as a partnership or corporation, recognized by law as having rights and duties, (7) a grammatical category, and (8) any of the three modes of being in the Trinity. Obviously, to use such a versatile word effectively, a clear and concise definition is needed.

For this study, when used in reference to the persons of the trinity, the word "person" will denote a self-conscious being with a unique and distinct personality, fully capable of sharing in a loving and intimate relationship with other like beings. It encompasses such aspects of personality as the mind, the will, and the emotions. This general definition of "divine" personality is just the beginning. I will gradually build upon it during the course of this investigation, and eventually use it as an integral part of the proposed theory.

God created human beings in his image (Gen. 1:26; 5:1; James 3:9). It then follows that there is significant similarity between divine personality and human personality, similarity that enables them to share an intimate relationship with one another. This being the case, there may be the tendency to define the persons of the trinity as glorified men. This must be avoided. Their similarity should not overshadow their difference. The persons of the trinity have a common uniqueness, a uniqueness that sets them apart from human beings. Ideally, a definition of the Father, the Son, and the Spirit as persons must strike the right balance, accounting for both the similarity and difference between divine and human personality. I will attempt to integrate just such a balanced definition of divine personality into the proposed solution.

Other important words used in this study are *knowledge* and *information*. The word *knowledge* refers to the possession of information. It is something actually known by someone. One's knowledge may be information acquired through observation. Or, it may be information acquired directly from God. This does not mean that one's knowledge is limited to information acquired from outside oneself. One can increase in knowledge, for example, through creative ideas, which stem from the imagination. The point is that knowledge refers to the possession of information regardless of the source.

The word *information* will have a particular meaning in this investigation. It is not a philosophical term that refers to something that does not exist or has never existed. Rather, it is grounded in reality; it deals with historical facts. Simply put, information is something true about creation.

In regard to creation, there are many different types of information. A material object, for example, provides qualitative information, such as size, weight, color, shape, and texture. There are other types of information that are not so easy to measure. Thoughts and emotions are two examples. Information about creation may fall into any one of the following general categories:

Dominions, principalities, kingdoms, authorities, governments, tribes, families, relationships, living things, angels, demons, personalities, natures, instincts, thoughts, imaginations, dreams, feelings, emotions, events, activities, actions, experiences, efforts, occupations, languages, solids, liquids, gases, elements, particles, materials, compounds, mixtures, structures, objects, colors, shapes, sizes, textures, patterns, densities, weights, viscosities, tastes, odors, sounds, dimensions, heights, depths, distances, spatial relations, perspectives, arrangements, wind, light, shadows, energies, powers, gravity, motion, temperatures, intensities, laws, principles, wisdom, etc.

It is clear from this partial list of categories that the amount of information that exists about creation is virtually infinite. If someone said, "I have all knowledge about creation for the present moment," that individual would need to possess all information in every category at that particular moment in time. If someone else said, "I have all knowledge about creation for all time," that individual would need to possess all information in every category at every moment in time, from the beginning of creation to the end of creation.

Time adds a great deal of complexity to the availability of information about creation. As time marches on, new information about creation is progressively revealed. A leaf pushed by the wind is in one location at one moment, and in another location the next. The present location of the leaf is new information about creation. The present location does not last long, however. With the passing of time, it quickly becomes a past location, and thus historical information. It is a continuous cycle—a possibility becomes a present reality, then a part of history. The present is perhaps best defined as that infinitesimal moment in time that separates the past from the future.

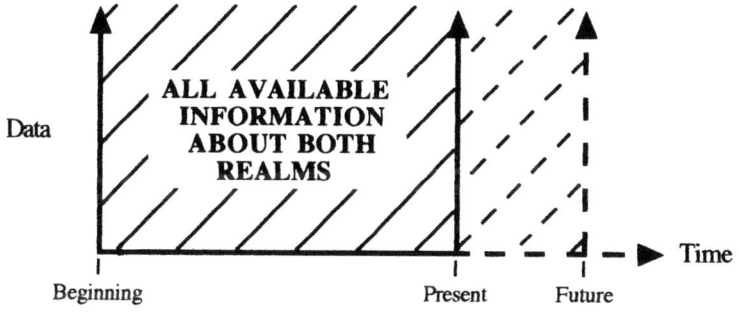

Figure 2: Realm Information

Lastly, a few words about *realms* are in order. There are two realms: the physical realm and the spiritual realm. The physical realm is our environment, where we exist as physical beings, while the spiritual realm is where spiritual beings exist, such as angels and demons. The latter domain includes heaven itself. Both realms co-exist together, separate and distinct, yet interrelated to one another. What happens in one realm affects the other. They are also time-related; the time in one realm is synchronized with the time in the other. The physical and spiritual realms together may be seen as two interrelated realities that encompass the whole of creation.

A key concept concerns the relationship between information and the physical and spiritual realms. Figure 2 is a graphic illustration of all the available information about both realms. The horizontal axis represents *time*.[1] From the beginning to the present moment is the past.[2] From the present moment forward is the future. The vertical axis represents *data*. Data is the smallest unit of any type of information. It should not be thought of as a unit of information that can be measured, but an infinitesimally small derivative of any type of information.

The shaded area from the beginning to the present moment—represented by the solid diagonal lines—is available information about both realms. This information includes every type of information that has existed (past) or currently exists (present) about creation. This information is called *available* information because, as far as time-based reality is concerned, it includes all that may be known about creation. Available information reflects the reality of what *was* and *is* concerning both realms.

The shaded area from the present moment to some future time—represented by the dashed diagonal lines—is unavailable information about both realms. This information does not exist as far as time-based reality is concerned. It becomes available when and only when the future becomes the present. Significantly, God alone possesses all yet-to-be-available information about creation; and when he chooses to share some of it with others, he is graciously providing prophetic insight into the future.

With the aid of these key words and concepts, I will develop a biblical understanding of the nature and function of the trinity, the "chassis" of the proposed theological system. With this end in mind, the remainder of this chapter will be organized into four general sections: Uniqueness and Superiority of God, Persons of the Trinity, Nature of the Trinity, and Monotheism and the Trinity.

B. Uniqueness and Superiority of God

From beginning to end, the Old Testament declares the uniqueness and superiority of God. Moses proclaimed to the people: "Know therefore today, and take it to your heart, that the Lord, He is God in heaven above and on the earth below; there is no other" (Deut. 4:39) and "Hear, O Israel! The Lord is our God, the Lord is one!" (6:4). In prayer, David said, "there is none like Thee, and there is no God beside Thee" (2 Sam. 7:22). Solomon echoed the thoughts of his father: "the Lord is God; there is no one else" (1 Kings 8:60). Unlike the nations that worshiped and served many gods, the children of Israel worshiped and served one and only one God.

The uniqueness and superiority of God is also found in the prophetic writings. In the Book of Isaiah, God himself states that he always has been and always will be one of a kind: "Before Me there was no God formed, and there will be none after Me" (Isa. 43:10). A bit later the same book records the following words of the Lord: "I am the first and I am the last, and there is no God besides Me" (44:6) and "I am the Lord, and there is none else" (45:18). The belief that there is one true God is a common thread woven throughout the tapestry of the entire Old Testament.

The God of Israel is clearly set apart from the gods of their neighbors. In fact, the God of Israel is the living God, while the other so-called gods are not gods at all. The Psalmist exclaimed, "For all the gods of the peoples are idols" (Ps. 96:5). They are products of the imagination, lifeless stone and metal, providing no benefit to those who worship them: "The idols of the nations are but silver and gold, the work of man's hands. They have mouths, but they do not speak; they have eyes, but they do not see; they have ears, but they do not hear; nor is there any breath at all in their mouths. Those who make them will be like them, yes, everyone who trusts in them" (135:15–18). Unlike the inanimate gods of the nations, the one true God is alive, active within creation and personally involved with his people.

The God of heaven is Creator, Sustainer, Savior, and the source of prophetic utterance. He made the heavens, the earth, and the seas and gives life to everything (Neh. 9:6). He also replenishes the earth: "Are there any among the idols of the nations who give rain? Or can the heavens grant showers? Is it not Thou, O Lord our God? Therefore we hope in Thee, for Thou art the one who has done all these things" (Jer. 14:22). He is the Savior who delivers his people from the hands of their oppressor (see Isa. 43:11). God is the source of all true prophecy. He declares "the end from the beginning, and from ancient times things which have not been done" (46:10). Who he is, what he has done, and what he continues to do sets him apart from all creation. He alone is worthy of worship and praise.

The New Testament writers did not believe that the God of the Old Testament had passed away. Neither did they believe that they were declaring salvation in another deity. Rather, they proclaimed that the God of their fathers had revealed a more complete revelation of himself and his ultimate plan for humanity, the long-awaited redemption he had promised in ages past. This being so, it should not be surprising that the New Testament writings reflect Old Testament themes.

Both the uniqueness and superiority of God are prominent themes in the New Testament. Paul wrote, "since indeed God who will justify the circumcised by faith and the uncircumcised through faith is one" (Rom. 3:30) and "Now a mediator is not for one party only; whereas God is only one" (Gal. 3:20). James wrote, "You believe that God is one. You do well; the demons also believe, and shudder" (James 2:19). Paul also contrasted the existence of the living God with idols: "we know that there is no such thing as an idol in the world, and that there is no God but one" (1 Cor. 8:4). See also John 5:44 and 1 Timothy 1:17. The Old Testament belief in the existence of a single God is clearly reaffirmed by the New Testament writers.

The New Testament writers had a definite continuity with the past. They held to the faith of their ancestors, that the Lord is one and there is no other. But in the process of doing so, they also introduced ideas that appear to contradict old beliefs. Some New Testament passages state that the Father alone is the one true God, while other passages refer to the Son with divine names, such as "God" and "Lord." Divine works such as creative acts, sustaining life, regeneration, and sanctification, which were once ascribed to the one true God in the old dispensation, are now ascribed to the Father and to the Son and to the Holy Spirit. Perhaps the most puzzling of all, worship, which was offered to God and to God alone, is now offered to Jesus.

On the surface, the evidence is somewhat of a mystery. From this point forward, I will begin the process of sorting things out. The next section will systematically analyze the biblical evidence concerning the persons of the trinity. I will begin with a brief study of possible allusions to divine plurality found in the Old Testament. The greater part of the next section will be spent in the New Testament, with the express purpose of providing a detailed sketch of divine personality. Eventually, this insight will be used in constructing a concept of the trinity.

C. Persons of the Trinity

As just shown, the uniqueness and superiority of the one true God is a major theme in both Testaments. In the earlier Testament, in particular, this theme is very pronounced. However, this strong monotheistic bent does not categorically dismiss the idea of divine plurality. The following are several prominent examples considered by some Christian scholars to be Old Testament allusions to the persons of the trinity. Since Old Testament references to the Son and the Spirit are less obvious and often difficult to interpret, our attention will be focused on passages that concern them.

God is identified as *Elohim*. *Elohim* is a plural noun, and some have seen a plurality of persons here. But it is perhaps best not to read too much into this. Most scholars today believe that this name refers to a plurality of excellence or majesty rather than the plurality of the trinity. Better yet are passages where God himself uses the plural pronouns *us* and *our:* "Let Us make man in Our image" (Gen. 1:26), "the man has become like one of Us" (3:22), "Come, let Us go down and there confuse their language" (11:7), and "Whom shall I send, and who will go for Us" (Isa. 6:8). Expressions such as these allude to a plurality of equals, a plurality that some Christian scholars interpret within the context of inter-trinitarian dialogue.

Some Old Testament creation passages highlight the activity of the *word* and the *spirit*. The Psalmist proclaimed that God's active word brought forth creation: "By the word of the Lord the heavens were made, and by the breath of His mouth all their host" (Ps. 33:6). Also, in the Genesis creation narrative, "the Spirit of God was moving over the surface of the waters" (1:2). In light of New Testament insight, where the "Word" is synonymous with Jesus (John 1:1,14; Rev. 19:13) and the Spirit takes on a personal dimension, some Christian scholars see these Old Testament passages as legitimate—though admittedly veiled—references to the second and third person of the trinity.

At times, a personal agent appears in the Old Testament who speaks as God (i.e., in the first person) and is addressed with divine names. For example, the angel of the Lord who appeared to Hagar in Genesis 16:7–13 spoke as God (v. 10). He is also referred to as "Lord" and "God" (v. 13). One of Abraham's three visitors was a similar figure who was repeatedly referred to as "the Lord" (Gen. 18:1, 10, 13, 22, 33). The angel of the Lord who prevented Abraham from sacrificing Isaac in Genesis 22:11–18 also spoke as God (vv. 12, 15–18). The one who appeared to Moses in the burning bush was an angel (Exod. 3:2), but he identified himself as "the God of Abraham, Isaac, and Jacob" (v. 6). And the figure who stood before Joshua and identified himself as the "captain of the host of the Lord" in Joshua 5:13–15 was referred to as "the Lord" (v. 14). Some Christian scholars interpret some or possibly all of these Old Testament figures as appearances of the preincarnate Christ.

A number of Old Testament prophecies point to a messianic figure who would arrive on the scene and visit God's people. Isaiah referred to a coming liberator as "Lord" and "God": "Clear the way for the Lord in the wilderness; make smooth in the desert a highway for our God" (Isa. 40:3). He also referred to him with the lofty titles of "Immanuel" (Isa. 7:14, later translated in Matthew as "God with us" (1.23)), Wonderful Counselor, Mighty God, Eternal Father, Prince of Peace (see Isa. 9:6).[3] Jeremiah called the coming king "The Lord our righteousness" (Jer. 23:6), and Malachi referred to a future messenger as "the Lord" (Mal. 3:1). These prophecies speak of a coming messianic figure in exalted terms, and some Christian scholars interpret them as allusions to Jesus and his divine identity.

Some Christian scholars believe that the Old Testament passages that personify wisdom point to the second person of the trinity (Prov. 3:19; 8:12–36). It is written of wisdom:

> The Lord possessed me at the beginning of His way, before His works of old. . . . When He established the heavens, I was there. . . . Then I was beside Him as a master workman; and I was daily His delight, rejoicing always before Him. . . . For blessed are they who keep my ways. . . . For he who finds me finds life, and obtains favor from the Lord (Prov. 8:22–35).

In light of the fact that the New Testament proclaims Jesus "the wisdom of God" (1 Cor. 1:24; cf. Col. 2:3), the connection between the Old Testament personification of wisdom and Jesus appears possible. It must be strongly emphasized, however, that these wisdom passages may be interpreted in more than one way. The people who lived during Old Testament times would not have understood the wisdom of God to be "a person to be addressed but only a personification of an attribute or activity of Yahweh."[4]

The Old Testament speaks of the Spirit as God's active agent who empowers God's servants for service, imparts wisdom and knowledge, and gives guidance and direction. The Messiah, referred to as the "Branch," will be equipped for ministry when the "Spirit of the Lord will rest on Him" (Isa. 11:1–2). Isaiah refers to the Spirit as God's Spirit: "And now the Lord God has sent Me [the

Messiah], and His Spirit" (48:16). Other like expressions include "My Spirit shall not strive with man forever" (Gen. 6:3), "The Spirit of God has made me" (Job 33:4), and "Thou dost send forth Thy Spirit" (Ps. 104:30). The emphasis here is clearly on the identification of the Spirit with God rather than the Spirit as a distinct personality, separate from God. Significantly, the prophet Micah implies that the Spirit may be provoked to anger (Mic. 2:7).

As mentioned earlier, the Old Testament's monotheistic bent does not categorically dismiss the idea of divine plurality. On the other hand, as the above evidence has shown, neither does it provide a clear reference to a divine Son or to an equally divine, personal Spirit. At best, the Old Testament points to divine figures who are content to remain in the shadows. Having said this, let's turn to the New Testament for illumination. The rest of this section will address the following topics: the distinction between the persons of the trinity, a description of divine personality, and a discussion of divine references and how they apply to each person of the trinity.

1. Distinction

Monarchianism was a third-century understanding of God, which attempted to safeguard the oneness of God. The proponents of this view feared that a God of three distinct persons would inevitably result in tritheism, severing all ties with the monotheism of the Old Testament. They also took things a step further and suggested several non-trinitarian alternatives. Modalistic monarchianism, or modalism, viewed the Father, the Son, and the Holy Spirit as three different modes or manifestations or phases of the same God. "Dynamic, or adoptionistic, monarchianism proposed a monotheism of God the Father in relation to which Jesus was viewed as a mere man who was endowed with the Holy Spirit."[5] In its various forms, monarchianism attempts to provide a rational explanation of the Father, the Son, and the Holy Spirit given that God is one person.

The proponents of monarchianism had a legitimate fear. Maintaining the unity of God is important. However, due to their overemphasis in this direction, critics felt they went too far and compromised significant portions of Scripture. In general, modalistic monarchianism, or modalism, neglects the distinction between the persons of the trinity, while dymanmic monarchianism does not account for the Son's unique personality. The error of the former theory will be addressed in this subsection, while the next subsection will address the deficiency of the latter.

The New Testament provides several key expressions that have trinitarian overtones. Perhaps the best known is the baptismal formula: "Go therefore and make disciples of all the nations, baptizing them in the name of the Father and the Son and the Holy Spirit" (Matt 28:19). Paul's closing words to the Corinthians include the following: "The grace of the Lord Jesus Christ, and the love of God, and the fellowship of the Holy Spirit, be with you all" (2 Cor. 13:14). Concerning redemption, Peter wrote, "according to the foreknowledge of God the Father, by the sanctifying work of the Spirit, that you may obey Jesus Christ and be sprinkled with His blood" (1 Peter 1:2). Additional passages that express a similar pattern are Romans 15:16, 2 Corinthians 1:21–22, Ephesians 2:18, 1 John 5:7–8[6], and Jude 20–21. These passages imply a distinction between the Father, the Son, and the Holy Spirit, a distinction that maintains a balance of equality, diversity, and order.

The distinction between the persons of the trinity is evident in several pivotal events in Jesus' life. His baptism is one example (Matt. 3:13–17; Mark 1:9–11; Luke 3:21–22). When Jesus was baptized in the Jordan River, heaven opened and the Spirit descended on him like a dove. Then a voice from heaven said, "This is My beloved Son, in whom I am well-pleased" (Matt. 3:17). The Father, the Son, and the Holy Spirit are all present and active at this event. Another relevant event took place on the Mount of Transfiguration, where the Father again audibly spoke to his Son (Matt. 17:1–9; Mark 9:2–10, Luke 9:28–36). These events are only intelligible when one assumes that several parties are interacting with one another, for to suggest that the speaker and the one spoken to are the same person is a peculiar interpretation indeed.

The baptism and transfiguration events reveal something more. The Father's words betray a certain quality of relationship, a relationship characterized by intimacy and love. Along these lines, John records the love the Father has for the Son (John 3:35; 5:20; 15:9; 17:24) and the Son for the Father (14:31). Such a relationship requires a lover and a beloved, love given and love received. The closeness between the Father, the Son, and the Spirit is underscored by the wording of other passages as well: the Father sent the Son (John 6:57), the Son prays to the Father (Luke 23:46), the Son sent the Spirit (John 16:7), the Spirit led the Son (Mark 1:12), and so forth. From a trinitarian perspective, these passages may be understood and interpreted within the context of a healthy relationship. Conversely, modalism does not acknowledge the existence of a relationship between the persons of the trinity; therefore, it must interpret these passages in some other fashion—perhaps they speak of some form of self-love!

Modalism also stumbles when viewed in relation to the basic meaning of words and their natural and normal function within a sentence. For example, John recorded the following words of Jesus: "When the Helper comes, whom I will send to you from the Father, that is the Spirit of truth, who proceeds from the Father, He will bear witness of Me" (John 15:26). The words *send* and *from* indicate that someone is moving away from someone else, and therefore they strongly suggest that more than one party is present. Other words also support this interpretation. Personal pronoun such as *I* and *he* don't normally refer to the same person in the same sentence. Once again, this passage, as well as others like it, demand that a personal distinction be made between the Father, the Son, and the Holy Spirit.

John records a clash between Jesus and the Pharisees (John 8:12–18). Some Pharisees challenged Jesus' claim to be "the light of the world," and they attempted to do so by using the Mosaic Law. According to the Law, two witnesses are required to validate a claim (Deut. 17:5–6; 19:15). Since these religious leaders presumed that Jesus was serving as the sole witness to his claim, they insisted that his claim was invalid. Jesus refuted their allegation. He said, "I am He who bears witness of Myself, and the Father who sent Me bears witness of Me" (John 8:18). According to modalism, the names *Father* and *Son* refer to the same person. If this assertion is true, the Pharisees were right. Jesus' claim was invalid because it was not substantiated by the testimony of two witnesses. On the other hand, a biblical understanding of the trinity allows

Jesus to make such a claim and satisfy the stipulation of the Law: Jesus is one witness, the Father is the other.

In light of the New Testament passages presented above, modalism and its claim that the Father, the Son, and the Holy Spirit are one and the same person is found wanting. The biblical witness clearly shows that they are distinct persons, who share in an intimate, loving relationship with one another. Next, to provide an antidote to dynamic monarchianism's claim that Jesus was a mere man filled with the Spirit, we will discuss what divine personality is like.

2. Description

Adam and Eve walked with God in the cool of the garden. They shared in a close and intimate relationship with their Creator. This relationship was possible because God created them like himself, in his own image and likeness (Gen. 1:26–27; 9:6). This subsection will begin by discussing some things that God and human beings share in common, including intellectual capabilities (e.g., perception, thinking, reasoning, understanding, and remembering), the power of volition, and the ability to show affection and express emotions. It will end by highlighting several key differences between divine and human personality. The objective will be to develop a properly balanced understanding of the persons of the trinity.[7]

In Scripture, it is not difficult to find examples of the Father and the Son exercising both intellect and volition. For example, the Father "so loved the world, that He gave His only begotten Son, that whoever believes in Him should not perish, but have eternal life" (John 3:16). The

Father formulated a plan according to his good pleasure and then acted upon it. The Son also participated in the process. He understood the Father's plan and voluntarily chose to do his Father's will. Jesus said, "For I have come down from heaven, not to do My own will, but the will of Him who sent Me" (6:38). This single example clearly illustrates the operation of the Father and the Son's intellectual as well as volitional faculties.

Both the Father and the Son expressed emotions. The Father expressed emotions such as compassion (James 5:11), hatred (Rom. 9:13), love (John 3:16; 2 Cor. 9:7; 1 John 4:16), and mercy (Phil. 2:27; James 5:11).[8] The Son expressed emotions such as agony (Luke 22:44), anger (Mark 3:5; John 2:15–16), astonishment (Matt. 8:10), compassion (Matt. 9:36; 14:14; 15:32; 20:34; Mark 6:34; 8:2; Luke 7:13), disgust (Matt. 17:17), distress (Mark 14:33; John 11:33), grief (Matt. 26:37, 38; Mark 14:34), joy (Luke 10:21), love (Mark 10:21; John 11:5; 13:1; 15:9; 19:26), sorrow (Matt. 23:37; Mark 8:12; Luke 19:41; John 11:35), and sympathy (Heb. 4:15).

The word *Spirit* conjures up the image of an impersonal force. However, the New Testament writers clearly identify the Holy Spirit as a distinct personality who thinks and wills and feels. Paul informed the Romans that he who searches our hearts (God) knows the mind of the Spirit, because the Spirit intercedes for the saints in accordance with God's will (Rom. 8:27). The Spirit searches the deep things of God (1 Cor. 2:10) and evaluates situations in order to make judgments as he sees fit (Acts 15:28). The Spirit is called "the Counselor," who will teach and guide believers (Luke 12:12; John 14:26; 16:13; 1 Cor. 2:13). The Spirit directed Peter to go with some men (Acts 11:12) and set apart and sent out Barnabas and Saul for missionary work (13:2–4). The Spirit forbade

Paul to speak the word in Asia (16:6) and later warned him of future hardships (20:23; 21:11). The Spirit distributes spiritual gifts as he wills (1 Cor. 12:11). The Spirit also encouraged (Acts 9:31), convicted (John 16:8), testified (John 15:26; Heb. 10:15), and witnessed (Acts 5:32; Rom. 8:16). In addition, the Holy Spirit expressed emotions such as grief (Eph. 4:30), offense (Heb. 10:29), and love (Rom. 15:30).

As this evidence shows, each person of the trinity expresses aspects of personality similar to our own, i.e., the mind, the will, and the emotions. On the other hand, divine personality is not identical to human personality. There are significant differences that must be considered and studied carefully. Moreover, not all differences are of the same kind, for some differences are by design, while others are due primarily to the current fallen state of human personality. In regard to the latter, Adam's sin has had a negative impact on all human faculties. Since the Fall, human personality has not functioned to its full potential. It always preforms short of the ideal. Some relevant differences of this kind are as follows.

Human beings understand little of what they know, and with the passing of time they forget much of what they have learned. But the persons of the trinity understand all that they know in the fullest possible way. They know themselves perfectly, and they understand all things according to their nature and design. They know the difference between light and darkness, truth and error, and never confuse one thing with another. All things are understood in their proper perspective. Additionally, they never forget what they know; they retain all information at all times.

Human beings have been given the privilege of exercising limited volitional freedom. However, they often find themselves powerless to do what they desire to do, and what they do frequently stems from improper motives. But the persons of the trinity exercise volitional freedom in harmony with their flawless character, and each decision is always based on an accurate assessment of all relevant information. As Scripture shows, their actions are always righteous, holy, just, and good; their motives are pure and undefiled; and they always choose the best possible course of action for all situations at all times to achieve the best possible results.

Human beings express emotions that are mixed and sometimes insincere. They often stem from fear, shame, or guilt. But the persons of the trinity express pure and natural emotions. Their emotions are always the proper and appropriate response to a given situation as well as an accurate indicator of what is felt at the time.

These examples highlight some differences between divine and human personality, which exist because of the fallen human condition. But, as mentioned earlier, other differences are differences by design. Several relevant differences of this kind are as follows.

Human beings are capable of engaging in one or, at most, several activities at any given moment in time. But the persons of the trinity have the multi-tasking capability that would exhaust the most sophisticated super-computer. They have the ability to observe all that takes place in creation and maintain such an awareness indefinitely without growing tired. They can also participate in an infinite number of activities and personal relationships simultaneously.

Human beings have intellectual limitations which prevent them from efficiently processing, storing, and accessing information. But the persons of the trinity have lightning-quick processing speed, unlimited storage capacity, and complete real-time access to stored data. They can learn all that can be learned; they can know all that can be known; and they always have plenty of room for additional input.

In summary, this subsection has outlined the nature of the persons of the trinity, showing that divine personality is similar, yet uniquely set apart and infinitely superior to human personality. Similarity encompasses like aspects of personality (mind, will, emotions), while difference includes superior function and design. Next, we will look at the persons of the trinity from a different angle, and discuss if and, if so, how each person is ascribed divine names, eternality, and divine works.

3. Divine References

Early in the fourth century, the church faced what it perceived to be a threatening dilemma. A theologian named Arius (d. 336) put forth a theory of Christ that suggested that he was the first and foremost created being. He is of a like substance to the Father, not the same substance as the Father.[9] In other words, Jesus is not God. Athanasius (d. 373), along with many other theologians, opposed Arius' claim. They believed that the Bible bears witness to the deity of Jesus Christ. In order to maintain peace within the empire, Emperor Constantine (d. 337) called the first ecumenical council to settle the dispute. At Nicaea in A.D. 325, the council convened to debate the matter. After days of deliberation, the consensus sided with Athanasius and his followers. The council affirmed that Jesus Christ is "very God of very God, begotten, not made, being of one substance with the Father."[10]

Some time later, Macedonianism emerged, a belief

that claims that the Spirit is inferior to the Father and the Son. Now, the Holy Spirit is seen as something less than God. A council at Constantinople met in A.D. 381 to clarify the church's position. The council stated that the Holy Spirit is "the Lord and Giver of life, who proceedeth from the Father, who with the Father and the Son together is worshipped and glorified."[11] The Council of Nicaea affirmed the deity of the Son, while the council at Constantinople affirmed the deity of the Holy Spirit. Did the early church make the right decisions? The following discussion will examine some of the pertinent biblical evidence.

Scripture ascribes divine *names* to the Father and the Son. The Father is referred to as God the Father (Gal. 1:1; Eph. 5:20), God and Father (Gal. 1:4; 1 Thess. 1:3; 3:13), God our Father (1 Cor. 1:3; Eph. 1:2; 2 Thess. 2:16), and Lord God Almighty (Rev. 11:17). The Son is referred to as God (John 1:1; 20:28; Rom. 9:5; Heb. 1:8), God and Savior (Titus 2:13; 2 Peter 1:1), true God and eternal life (1 John 5:20), and Immanuel, which means God with us (Matt. 1:23). Jesus was frequently called the Son of God (e.g., Matt. 8:29; Mark 3:11; John 1:34; 11:27; 20:31). He also claimed this name for himself (Luke 22:70). Significantly, on several occasions when he did so, some Jews tried to stone him for blasphemy (Matt. 26:65; Mark 14:64; John 5:18; 10:33–36). Jesus' claim to be the Son of God was perceived as a claim to be equal with God (John 5:18; cf. 10:33).

The Spirit is not called "God" in the New Testament. However, there is one possible exception found in the Book of Acts (5:3–4). When Ananias attempted to deceive the apostles concerning the proceeds from a sale of property, Peter said, "Ananias, why has Satan filled your heart to lie to the Holy Spirit, and to keep back some of the price of the land? . . . You have not lied to men, but to God." Peter may be implying that the Spirit is God, though such an interpretation is questionable. More than likely, he is simply saying that lying to the Spirit is an affront to God.

In the New Testament writings, the Greek word *kurios* is used as a title of respect, often translated "Sir" (e.g., Matt. 13:27). But sometimes it is translated "Lord" and appears to favor a title. This usage speaks of divine function rather than divine being. Along these lines are passages that state that Jesus was made Lord (i.e., assumed sovereign rule), a lordship bestowed upon him by virtue of his resurrection (e.g., Acts 2:36; Rom. 14:9). In its highest usage, *kurios* is once again translated "Lord," but now serves as a virtual synonym for "God," the most explicit examples being where the New Testament quotes the Old Testament, substituting the Hebrew *yahweh* with the Greek *kurios*. Both the Father (e.g., Matt. 22:44, cf. Ps. 110:1) and the Son (e.g., Matt. 3:3, cf. Isa. 40:3; Heb. 1:10, cf. Ps. 102:2) are referred to in this way. The Spirit is not called "Lord" in the New Testament; though, admittedly, Paul comes very close on one occasion (see 2 Cor. 3:17–18).

Scripture ascribes *eternality* to each person of the trinity. For this study, eternality is defined as conscious and unchanging existence from everlasting to everlasting (see Ps. 90:2).[12] Paul called the Father the eternal God (Rom. 16:26). He was also described as the one "who is and who was and who is to come" (Rev. 1:4). The Son was in the beginning (John 1:1) and existed before all things (Col. 1:17; cf. John 17:5, 24). He was revealed as the Living One, who will live forever and ever (Rev. 1:18). Jesus was referred to as the "Alpha and Omega, the first and the last, the beginning and the end" (Rev. 22:13; cf. 1:8;

21:6). He also referred to himself as *I am* in one form or another (e.g., John 8:24, 28, 58), a somewhat ambiguous phrase, which most likely alludes to never-ending existence. The author of Hebrews referred to the Holy Spirit as the "Eternal Spirit" (Heb. 9:14). Jesus stated that the Counselor (i.e., Holy Spirit) will be with believers forever (John 14:16).

Scripture ascribes divine *works* to each person of the trinity. For example, all three persons are involved in creative acts. Paul clearly stated that the Father and the Son created all things: "yet for us there is but one God, the Father, from whom are all things, and we exist for Him; and one Lord, Jesus Christ, by whom are all things, and we exist through Him" (1 Cor. 8:6; cf. Heb. 1:2). John wrote of the Son, "All things came into being by Him, and apart from Him nothing came into being that has come into being" (John 1:3). Paul again expressed the Son's creative involvement: "For by Him all things were created, both in the heavens and on earth, visible and invisible, whether thrones or dominions or rulers or authorities—all things have been created by Him and for Him" (Col. 1:16). The Spirit was present and active during the creation event (Gen. 1:2). The Psalmist exclaimed, "Thou dost send forth Thy Spirit, they are created" (Ps. 104:30). The Book of Job also expresses the creative involvement of the Spirit: "The Spirit of God has made me, and the breath of the Almighty gives me life" (33:4). The biblical writers show that all three persons of the trinity actively participate in creative acts.

All three persons of the trinity are involved in sustaining life. It is the Father "who gives life to all things" (1 Tim. 6:13), and his breath sustains life and renews "the face of the ground" (Ps. 104:29–30). If the Father were to remove his spirit and his breath, "all flesh would perish together, and man would return to dust" (Job 34:15). The Son holds all things together (Col. 1:17), upholding "all things by the word of His power" (Heb. 1:3). In Genesis, the Lord said: "My Spirit shall not strive with man forever, because he also is flesh" (Gen. 6:3). Life on earth would cease to exist apart from the active support of the Father, the Son, and the Holy Spirit.

All three persons of the trinity were involved in the incarnation of the Christ-child. The Father "prepared" a body for his Son (Heb. 10:5). The Son "who, although He existed in the form of God, did not regard equality with God a thing to be grasped, but emptied Himself, taking the form of a bond-servant, and being made in the likeness of men" (Phil. 2:6–7). The Christ-child was conceived of the Holy Spirit (Matt. 1:20). The angel Gabriel told Mary: "The Holy Spirit will come upon you, and the power of the Most High will overshadow you; and for that reason the holy offspring shall be called the Son of God" (Luke 1:35). In regard to the incarnation, the Father prepared, the Son emptied, and the Spirit conceived.

All three persons of the trinity were involved in the resurrection of Christ. More than a few passages credit the Father with his Son's resurrection (e.g., Acts 2:24, 32; 3:15; 4:10; 5:30; 10:40; 13:30; 17:31; Rom. 4:24; 6:4; 1 Cor. 15:15; Eph. 1:20; Col. 2:12; 1 Thess. 1:10; 1 Pet 1:21). Jesus declared that he will raise himself from the dead: "Destroy this temple, and in three days I will raise it up" (John 2:19, see v. 21). John later recorded the following words of Jesus. "For this reason the Father loves Me, because I lay down My life that I may take it again" (10:17). The Spirit also raised Jesus from the dead. Paul wrote, "who was declared the Son of God with power by the resurrection from the dead, according to the spirit of holiness, Jesus Christ our Lord" (Rom. 1:4) and "But if the

Spirit of Him who raised Jesus from the dead dwells in you, He who raised Christ Jesus from the dead will also give life to your mortal bodies through His Spirit who indwells you" (8:11). Peter wrote that Christ was "put to death in the flesh, but made alive in the spirit" (1 Peter 3:18).

All three persons of the trinity are involved in regeneration. Peter wrote: "Blessed be the God and Father of our Lord Jesus Christ, who according to His great mercy has caused us to be born again to a living hope through the resurrection of Jesus Christ from the dead" (1 Peter 1:3). The Son is also an indispensable factor in regeneration. John recorded the following words of Jesus: "I am the way, and the truth, and the life; no one comes to the Father, but through Me" (John 14:6). Jesus said of the Spirit: "Truly, truly, I say to you, unless one is born of water and the Spirit, he cannot enter into the kingdom of God. That which is born of the flesh is flesh, and that which is born of the Spirit is spirit" (3:5–6). All three are seen as active participants in regeneration in the following words: "He [the Father] saved us, not on the basis of deeds which we have done in righteousness, but according to His mercy, by the washing of regeneration and renewing by the Holy Spirit, whom He poured out upon us richly through Jesus Christ our Savior" (Titus 3:5–6).

All three persons of the trinity are involved in sanctification. Paul wrote: "Now may the God [the Father] of peace Himself sanctify you entirely; and may your spirit and soul and body be preserved complete, without blame at the coming of our Lord Jesus Christ" (1 Thess. 5:23). Paul wrote of the Son: "Husbands, love your wives, just as Christ also loved the church and gave Himself up for her; that He might sanctify her, having cleansed her by the washing of water with the word, that He might present to

Himself the church in all her glory, having no spot or wrinkle or any such thing; but that she should be holy and blameless" (Eph. 5:25–27). Paul also declared that the Spirit sanctifies believers (Rom. 15:16; cf. 1 Cor. 6:11; 2 Thess. 2:13; 1 Peter 1:2).

Scripture ascribes *worship* to the Father and the Son. Jesus said to the woman at the well: "But an hour is coming, and now is, when the true worshipers shall worship the Father in spirit and truth; for such people the Father seeks to be His worshipers" (John 4:23). Paul said that he bows his "knees before the Father" (Eph. 3:14). Like the Father, the Son was also worshiped. He was worshiped by the wise men (Matt. 2:11), a healed blind man (John 9:38), the disciples (Matt. 14:33; 28:17; Acts 13:2), women at the tomb (Matt. 28:9), and angels (Heb. 1:6). In Revelation, the Father and the Son are worshiped by multitudes (Rev. 5:13–14). The Holy Spirit is not worshiped in the New Testament, although some have argued that the Spirit's presence (i.e., "seven Spirits") before the heavenly throne implies that he too receives worship (Rev. 1:4; 5:6), and that Paul ascribed a form of worship to the Spirit when he included him in a benediction (2 Cor. 13:14).

This concludes this section on the persons of the trinity. The main points may be summarized as follows: (1) the Father, the Son, and the Holy Spirit are distinct persons who exercise aspects of personality such as the mind, the will, and the emotions, (2) divine personality is similar, yet uniquely set apart and infinitely superior to human personality, (3) the Father and the Son are ascribed divine names and worship (the evidence in regard to the Spirit is scant and unclear), and (4) all three persons of the trinity are ascribed eternality and divine works. Building upon what we have learned thus far, the next section will discuss the relationship between the persons of the trinity.

D. Nature of the Trinity

The filial relationship between the Father and the Son provides valuable insight concerning the nature of the trinity. To understand this relationship, it is necessary to see it in respect to two very important words. Jesus was referred to as the "firstborn." The Greek word for firstborn is *prototokos*. It is used in connection with Christ and creation (Col. 1:15), Christ and the resurrection (Col. 1:18; Rev. 1:5), Christ and the church (Rom. 8:29), and Christ and his second advent (Heb. 1:6). While Colossians 1:15 and Hebrews 1:6 undoubtedly allude to the Son's unique relationship with the Father, they unfortunately say little about the relationship itself. Perhaps the best we can glean from these passages is that this relationship affords the Son a special status with its privileges and responsibilities.

Jesus was also referred to as the "only begotten" Son. The Greek word for "only begotten" is *monogenes,* a compound word formed from *monos,* meaning first or only, and *genes,* meaning offspring. It is used several times in reference to Christ (John 1:14, 18; 3:16, 18; 1 John 4:9), and to describe Isaac's relationship to Abraham (Heb. 11:17). In John's writings, this word clearly refers to the Son's unique relationship to the Father. But I also believe that it points beyond this to something ontological in flavor: the Son's origin in the Father. Though it is not possible to prove this "begetting" beyond a doubt, nor is it possible to offer a precise definition of it, the following is nevertheless my particular understanding of this seminal event.[13]

First, the begetting of the Son was a real and objective act. The begetting of the Son does not refer to the birth of the Christ-child in first-century Bethlehem. Perhaps it is best seen in the following words of Jesus: "For just as the Father has life in Himself, even so He gave to the Son also to have life in Himself" (John 5:26). While the *how* of this exchange may elude us, one particular *what* is relatively clear: the Father gave the Son life in himself, and this gift of life speaks of the Son's origin in the Father.[14]

Second, the begetting of the Son was a timeless act. The begetting of the Son did not take place within the continuum of time-relative events. Neither was it the first event that signaled the beginning of time. In both cases, the Son would be a part of creation; and, as such, the best he could be is what Arius claimed him to be—the first and foremost created being. To avoid this conclusion, the begetting of the Son must be seen as an act that took place before the "beginning" (Gen. 1:1), outside the time-space reality in which we live. Only then could he be classified a truly eternal being, separate and distinct from creation.

Third, the begetting of the Son was a willed act. The creation story sets forth a universal axiom of creaturely procreation: living things procreate according to their own kind. Plants bring forth plants, animals bring forth animals, and humans bring forth humans, each according to their physical design. Each kind reproduces to bring forth similar offspring. Like creaturely procreation, the begetting of the Son did "bring forth" a similar kind, for both the Father and the Son are the same quality of person. However, unlike creaturely procreation, this begetting does not include some form of mating between like kinds. The Father willed the Son into existence, a timeless event that brought forth a purely spiritual being.

Fourth, the begetting of the Son was a unique act. The Son is the *only* begotten Son of the Father. There was no other like him, there is no other like him, and there never will be another like him. In light of his unparalleled origin, he is the only one who can call God his "natural" Father. All others become a son or daughter of God by way of adoption.

Finally, the begetting of the Son established a fixed and permanent relationship between the Father and the Son. The Father will always be the Father, and the Son will always be the Son. Their relationship to one another will always remain that of a Father to his Son and a Son to his Father. The eternal, unchanging Father and the eternal, unchanging Son share in an eternal, unchanging relationship.

Like the relationship between the Father and the Son, the relationship between the Father and the Spirit is illumined by a very important Greek word: *ekporeuomai*. While *ekporeuomai* is found throughout the New Testament, we are concerned here with one particular usage found in John's Gospel: "the Spirit of truth, who proceeds [*ekporeuomai*] from the Father" (John 15:26). Here, the basic meaning of *ekporeuomai* is "goes out from" (NIV). Like "begotten," I believe that it carries with it the idea of origin. But unlike "begotten," which points to a completed act, "procession" favors an ongoing happening, a happening that continues to this very day. Certainly, there is a potential danger here. As with the Spirit in general, there may be a tendency towards depersonalization. Procession is the sending forth of the Holy Spirit, a personal agent who has all aspects of divine personality.

While the Father's role in the Spirit's procession is rather straightforward ("from the Father"), the Son's role is not so well defined. Does the Spirit proceed from the Father alone or from the Father and the Son? Historically, Eastern Christendom favors the former interpretation, while Western the latter. Early on the church did not take a hard stand on this issue. Things changed when, to the dismay of the East, the clause *and from the Son,* referred to as the *filioque,* was inserted in the Nicene Creed at the Council of Toledo in A.D. 589. Despite repeated attempts to reach doctrinal agreement, the East and West eventually divided over this issue in A.D. 1054. They have remained divided ever since. Consequently, the church today has no consensus view in regard to the procession of the Spirit.

Having said this, I would like to go to the biblical text and make some general observations about the Spirit's procession. These insights will then be used to formulate a definition of the procession of the Spirit.

First, the Father sent the Spirit. Jesus said to the disciples, "If you then, being evil, know how to give good gifts to your children, how much more shall your heavenly *Father give the Holy Spirit* to those who ask Him?" (Luke 11:13, italics added). He later said, "And I will ask the Father, and *He will give you another Helper* [the Spirit]" (John 14:16, italics added). Paul wrote, "And because you are sons, *God has sent forth the Spirit* of His Son into your hearts, crying, 'Abba! Father!'" (Gal. 4:6, italics added).

Second, the Son received the Spirit from the Father. Jesus said, "When the Helper [the Spirit] comes, whom I will send to you *from the Father"* (John 15:26, italics added). On the day of Pentecost, Peter stated that the Son received the Spirit from the Father: "Therefore having been exalted to the right hand of God, and having *received from the Father* the promise of the Holy Spirit, He has poured forth this which you both see and hear" (Acts 2:33, italics added).

Finally, the Son sent the Spirit. Jesus said, "When the Helper [the Spirit] comes, whom *I will send* to you from the Father" (John 15:26, italics added) and "but if I go, *I will send Him* [the Spirit] to you" (16:7, italics added). On one occasion, Jesus discharged the Spirit to the disciples (20:22). He also imparted the Spirit on the Day of Pentecost. Jesus said to his disciples, "And behold, *I am sending forth the promise* of My Father upon you; but you are to stay in the city until you are clothed with power from on high" (Luke 24:49, italics added). Peter also credits the Son with the outpouring of the Spirit (Acts 2:33).

The biblical evidence reveals several insights that help to explain the procession of the Spirit. Both the Father and the Son send forth the Spirit; however, they do not send forth the Spirit in the same way. The Father imparts the Spirit to the Son, then the Son imparts the Spirit. Or, stated a bit differently, the Father is the originator of the Spirit, while the Son is the mediator of the Spirit. In this context, the phrase *from the Father through the Son* provides as equitable definition of the Spirit's procession.

1. Ontological Order

As discussed above, the procession of the Spirit may be summarized as follows: the Spirit proceeds from the

```
      FATHER
        ▲
      HOLY
       SON
      SPIRIT
        ▼
```

Figure 3: The Ontological Order

Father through the Son. This basic definition is graphically illustrated in figure 3. For this study, this arrangement will be referred to as the *ontological order*.[15]

Figure 3 shows how the persons of the trinity are oriented in reference to one another. It does not describe how the persons of the trinity choose to function at a particular time, but how they have always and will always relate to one another. It is an eternal reality established before the creation of time, space, and matter, a fundamental and unalterable truth about the trinity that will not change under any and all circumstances.

The Father, the Son, and the Holy Spirit participate in an ongoing, dynamic relationship in keeping with the pattern of the ontological order: the Father relates to the Son by the Spirit, and the Son relates to the Father by the Spirit. This arrangement embraces personal as well as corporate distinctives.

In a *personal* sense, the persons of the trinity each operate according to the full perfection of divine personality. Their intellectual capabilities, such as perception, thinking, reasoning, understanding, and remembering, are unhindered and unlimited. Each person exercises the power of volition, which includes the ability to act according to one's good pleasure and choose between alternatives based on one's best judgment. Also, they express pure and natural emotions, which are always the proper and appropriate response to a given situation as well as an accurate indicator of what is felt at the time. Perfect love, joy, peace, patience, kindness, goodness, faithfulness, gentleness, and self-control are the rule here (cf. Gal. 5:23).

In a *corporate* sense, the persons of the trinity are a close-knit community. Several aspects of this community warrant special attention. First, it is a fellowship of intimacy. The persons of the trinity share their innermost thoughts and feelings with one another. At all times the lines of communication are open and unhindered. Jesus said, "For the Father loves the Son, and shows Him all things that He Himself is doing" (John 5:20). Paul wrote concerning the Spirit, "for the Spirit searches all things, even the depths of God. . . . so the thoughts of God no one knows except the Spirit of God" (1 Cor. 2:10–11). Truly, the persons of the trinity share in an intimate relationship at the deepest level.

Second, it is a fellowship of administrative order. The ontological order assumes a hierarchical structure. Scripture echoes this reality. For example, Paul wrote, "Christ is the head of every man, and the man is the head of a woman, and *God is the head of Christ*" (1 Cor. 11:3, italics added). As the husband assumes the place of headship in a marriage relationship, so the Father assumes a place of headship in relation to the Son and the Spirit. Thus we see the Father commit all things to the Son (John 3:35) and highly exalt him with a name that is above every name (Phil. 2:9). In this context, the Son can say "the Father is greater than I" (John 14:28). This claim in no way suggests that the Father is ontologically superior to the Son. As the husband's place of authority in the household does not make him genetically superior to his wife, so the Father's place of authority over the Son and the Spirit does not make him a superior person.

Finally, it is a fellowship of diversity and harmony. Each person of the trinity performs a variety of unique functions. For example, the Father fixed seasons and times (Acts 1:7), the Son became flesh and died for the sins of the world, and the Holy Spirit indwells and empowers believers. This variety is not at the expense of harmony. Jesus said, "for I always do the things that are pleasing to Him [the Father]" (John 8:29). The Son is not coerced to comply with a demand, but instead he willingly obeys the Father's request. The Father, the Son, and the Holy Spirit relate to one another in a spirit of willing cooperation, mutual respect, and self-giving love.

In summary, the persons of the trinity are a close-knit community characterized by intimacy, order, diversity, and harmony—the paradigm of all true fellowship.

A final word must be said about how the persons of the trinity communicate with one another. In the following examples, I will describe this conversation in a progressive manner. In reality, however, the logistics of this exchange are much more complex. The role of the Holy Spirit in the communication process is somewhat ambiguous and difficult to visualize. The Spirit "links up" the Father and the Son; but as a single, undivided, personal spirit who transcends spatial boundaries, he does so while being always-present with the Father and the Son.

Thus the Spirit does not need to travel to deliver information. Consequently, when the Father provides the Spirit with information, it becomes immediately accessible to the Son; and when the Son provides the Spirit with information, it becomes immediately accessible to the Father. In this light, the conversation between the persons of the trinity may best be understood as a progressive yet instantaneous exchange.

It is important to note that this particular form of communication is not confined to the trinity proper, but extends to wherever the Spirit is present. The Spirit also links up the Father and the Son with creation, thus enabling a time-free form of communication throughout both realms.

With this in mind, the following examples will help to clarify how the ontological order operates, both internally and with others outside its immediate circle of fellowship.

Figure 4 illustrates the progression of a prophetic word from the Father to a prophet. The Father is the originator of the message. Peter wrote, "But know this first of all, that no prophecy of Scripture is a matter of one's own interpretation, for no prophecy was ever made by an act of human will, but men moved by the Holy Spirit spoke from God" (2 Peter 1:20–21). Luke said the same thing when he wrote that God spoke by the Holy Spirit through the mouth of David (Acts 4:25). In a real sense, the Father "breathes" out the content of the message (see 2 Tim. 3:16).

The Son serves to mediate the message. Like any other mediator who supports the communication process between two parties, the Son supports the communication process between the Father to the prophet. What the Son receives from the Father he faithfully passes on; but in the process of doing so, he leaves his mark of love and

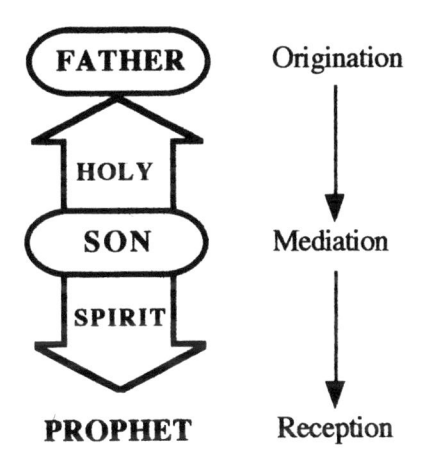

```
      FATHER         Origination
        ↑               │
      HOLY              │
       SON           Mediation
      SPIRIT            │
        ↓               │
                        ↓
     PROPHET         Reception
```

Figure 4: The Progression of Prophecy

compassion on the message itself. As a result, the Father's message is now the Son's message, while the Son's message remains the Father's message.

The person of the Holy Spirit serves to facilitate the transmission of the message from the Father, through the Son, and to its final destination. Jesus explains the role of the Spirit:

> I have many more things to say to you, but you cannot bear them now. But when He, the Spirit of truth, comes, He will guide you into all the truth; for He will not speak on His own initiative, but whatever He hears, He will speak; and He will disclose to you what is to come. He shall glorify Me; for He shall take of Mine, and shall disclose it to you. All things that the Father has are Mine; therefore I said, that He takes of Mine, and will disclose it to you (John 16:12–15).

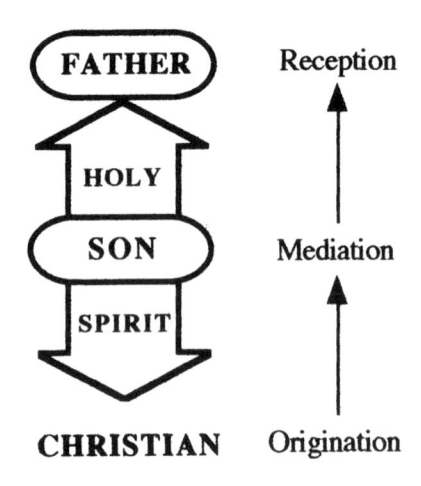

```
        FATHER        Reception
          ▲              ▲
        HOLY            │
         SON         Mediation
        SPIRIT          ▲
          ▼             │
      CHRISTIAN     Origination
```

Figure 5: The Progression of Prayer

The Spirit also ensures that the message is received properly. The Spirit engages the prophet's heart and mind in such a way that he is literally "moved" along by the Spirit (2 Peter 1:21). When all is said and done, the message may be rightly proclaimed "the word of the Lord."

In accord with the ontological order, the Father is originator of the prophetic word, the Son mediates it, and the Spirit delivers it to the prophet.

Figure 5 illustrates the progression of a prayer from a Christian to the Father. The believer is the originator of the prayer, although the Spirit may provide assistance (see Rom. 8:26). In accord with the ontological order, the Spirit makes the believer's request available to the other persons of the trinity. He intercedes for the believer according to the will of God (Rom. 8:27). The fact that the Spirit *intercedes* shows that he is more than a communication link, but personally involved in the process.

The Son serves to mediate the prayer. Paul wrote, "Christ Jesus is He who died, yes, rather who was raised, who is at the right hand of God, who also intercedes for us" (Rom. 8:34). The writer of Hebrews declared that the Son "is able to save forever those who draw near to God through Him, since He always lives to make intercession for them" (Heb. 7:25). Christ is an "advocate," who comes alongside the believer to argue his case (see 1 John 2:1). The prayer of the believer becomes the prayer of the Son, and the Son is sure to present the prayer in the most effective manner possible.

By the Spirit, the Son presents the prayer to the Father; and the Father decides what should be the appropriate response. Ultimately, his response is always in keeping with his benevolent character.

Of course, I have described the progression of a single prayer. In reality, thousands of prayers are offered up to the heavenly Father at any given moment in time. The Father hears them all, and he answers each one in the best possible way as he works out all things for the good of his children (Rom. 8:28).

These examples show how the Father, the Son, and the Holy Spirit operate according to the pattern of the ontological order. This "pattern of operation" is the same for all divine works. It must be kept in mind that the specifics of how the persons of the trinity relate to one another, how they process multiple events simultaneously, and how the Spirit works in the heart and mind of a human being is not clear. There are hidden mysteries to this reality, which remain beyond the reach of human imagination.

2. Omnipresence & Imminence

God spoke through the prophet: " 'Am I a God who is near,' declares the Lord, 'and not a God far off? Can a man hide himself in hiding places, so I do not see him?' declares the Lord. 'Do I not fill the heavens and the earth?' declares the Lord" (Jer. 23:23–24). The prophet proclaimed a profound truth: the God who transcends creation is also imminent in it. The New Testament witness echoes this reality. The God who dwells in "unapproachable light" (1 Tim. 6:16) is ever-present and fully aware of all that takes place within both realms.

But how does God "fill" the heavens and the earth? This is a difficult question to answer. God is invisible, yet always present and active in all things. Paul affirmed that "in Him [God] we live and move and exist" (Acts 17:28). He also wrote that God is "through all and in all" (Eph. 4:6) while sustaining all things. Steven Charnock provides helpful insight: "He compasseth all, is encompassed by none; He fills all, is comprehended by none. The Creator contains the world, the world contains not the Creator; as the hollow of the hand contains the water, the water in the hollow of the hand contains not the hand; and therefore some have chosen to say, rather that the world is in God, it lives and moves in Him, than that God is in the world."[16]

Christian theology has traditionally walked a narrow line between two poles. On the one hand, it denies pantheism. Pantheism is the idea "that God is really the substance of all things and that He is spatial."[17] On the other hand, it denies deism. Deism is the idea "that God is omnipresent in power but not in a personal sense."[18] Most conservative theologians hold to a balanced position: God is both distinct from his creation yet, at the same time, personally present, sustaining all things by his power.

Although God is present everywhere, he is not present everywhere in the same way. Herman Bravinck explains: "God's imminence is not an unconscious imminence, but a conscious presence of His being in all creatures. That is the reason why the nature of the divine presence varies in accordance with the nature of these creatures. To be sure, even the most insignificant creature owes its origin and preservation to God's power, to His being: God dwells in every creature; but this does not mean that He dwells equally in every creature. All things are indeed '*in* Him' but all things are not '*with* Him.' "[19] God dwells in a rock, a flower, a dog, and a human being; but only in the latter does he desire to reveal himself in a truly intimate way.

There is much about omnipresence that remains an enigma. However, the Bible is quite clear in regard to the location of each person of the trinity. The Father resides in heaven (e.g., Matt. 5:16; 6:9; 16:17; 18:10; 23:9). Before the incarnation, the Son dwelt in heaven with the Father (e.g., John 3:13; 6:62; 8:23; 16:27–28), and after his resurrection the Son returned to heaven to be seated at the right hand of the Father (e.g., Acts 7:55; Eph. 1:20; Col. 3:1; Heb. 1:3; 8:1; 10:12; 12:2; 1 Peter 3:22). (The location of the Son during his earthly life will be discussed in the next chapter.) The Psalmist exclaimed, "Where can I go from Thy Spirit? Or where can I flee from Thy presence?" (Ps. 139:7). The Holy Spirit is the personal presence of the trinity who permeates all creation (e.g., 1 Cor. 3:16; Eph. 2:22; 3:16).

Figure 6 illustrates the omnipresence of the trinity before Christ's incarnation and after his resurrection. The Father and the Son are located in heaven (which is

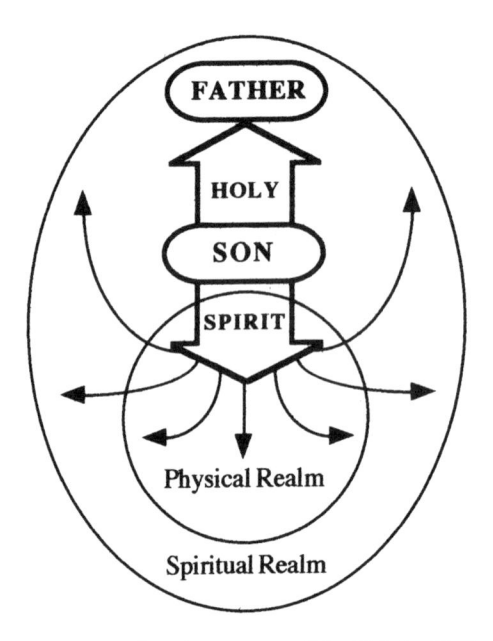

Figure 6: The Omnipresence of the Trinity Before Christ's Incarnation and After His Resurrection

somewhere in the spiritual realm), while the Holy Spirit permeates the whole of creation (or both realms). Thus there is a trinitarian presence everywhere in creation.

This figure also illustrates how each person of the trinity interacts with creation. In accord with the ontological order, the Spirit, who permeates all creation, encounters all that occurs in creation, and he makes his firsthand knowledge accessible to the others. In this way the Holy Spirit serves as the Father and the Son's spiritual "senses," the means by which they observe and participate in the affairs of everyday life.[20]

In regard to the exchange of information between the persons of the trinity, the Holy Spirit acquires the sum total of all present information about creation the moment it becomes available, and he makes it instantaneously accessible to the Father and the Son. Since this modus operandi has been in effect from the beginning of creation to the present, each person of the trinity has had complete access to and therefore complete possession of all available information about both realms.

It is important to note that this discussion has been limited to acquiring information about creation from within creation. From this time-based perspective, only past and present information may be known; future information is simply not available.

E. Monotheism and the Trinity

At this point, I would like to turn to one of the most perplexing and controversial topics in Christian theology—the monotheism question. Two biblical truths present themselves in apparent contrast to one another. First, the Old and New Testament writers proclaim the reality of a single God. And second, the New Testament writers refer to the Father as God and to the Son as God. These two statements create an obvious dilemma: how can the belief in one God be reconciled with two persons called God? In addition, the person of the Holy Spirit must also be considered. How does he fit into the picture? These questions have challenged many sincere truth-seekers throughout the centuries. It is perhaps most appropriate to begin in the fourth century when such things took center stage.

Many ideas about God were floating around in the fourth century. Some were biblical, some were questionable, and others missed the mark completely. Prominent theologians believed that the time was right to put their heads together to formulate a solution that the majority could agree upon. Using language and concepts that were familiar, they endeavored to bridge the gap between the biblical evidence and metaphysics to show that God is one ontological being consisting of three persons. After years of theological dialogue, the church majority resolved to define the one true God as *three persons of one substance*.[21] In other words, "God is a unitary essence consisting of three coequal persons—Father, Son, and Holy Spirit."[22] This understanding of God as trinity is thought to affirm the unity of God (one substance) as well as the plurality necessary for self-expression and intimate fellowship (three persons).

This definition of the trinity has found its place in history, serving as the standard of orthodoxy throughout the years. This does not mean that everyone agrees with it, however. It does raise some questions of its own. The fourth-century theologians borrowed the word *substance* from the world of philosophy, and some have questioned this. Others have questioned the metaphysical approach altogether, finding no justification for it in the Bible. Certainly, cultural context plays a major role here. The fourth-century theologians sought a biblically accurate solution that made sense to them and to their contemporaries. It is, therefore, a culturally conditioned solution, which is best understood in the context from which it came. It is not, in my opinion, an axiomatic solution binding on all Christians at all times.

I agree with the fourth-century theologians on the following point: the God of Abraham, Isaac, and Jacob was also the God of Matthew, Mark, Luke, and John. I differ with them in how this reality should be expressed in regard to divine oneness. The remainder of this section will outline my particular view at this time.

1. Jewish Roots

The theologians of the fourth century began with the deity of Jesus Christ and then set out to redefine monotheism. I will start in a different place and offer a different solution. Rather than start with what was said about Jesus, I will begin with what Jesus said about God. Did Jesus teach that he is the one true God? Or, did he teach that he has a God, the heavenly Father? My assumption here is that Jesus did not affirm both propositions, that he *is* God and he *has* a God. Consequently, it is necessary to make a choice between the two, one way or the other. In the following discussion, I will side with the idea that Jesus has a God, and that he embraced a belief in the God and monotheism that was consistent with what was taught in the synagogues of his day.

Jesus' monotheism, then, was a Jewish monotheism, a belief in God that is grounded in the Old Testament. Like Moses, David, and Solomon before him, Jesus believed in one God. To him, God is the God of heaven and the God of earth, the God of Israel, and the only true and living God. He is Creator, Sustainer, Savior, and the source of prophetic utterance. And he alone is worthy of worship and praise. It perhaps could go without saying, but it must be said for emphasis and clarity, that this monotheism is an *absolute* monotheism, a monotheism in which God has just one personality. To suggest otherwise is to move beyond the bounds of Old Testament monotheism and into territory completely foreign to the Judaism of Jesus' day.

Of course, beginning here, that Jesus has a God and that he embraced Jewish monotheism, the burden rests upon my shoulders to adequately account for those passages that refer to Jesus with divine names. Let's now turn to the New Testament and see what it has to say about divine oneness.

2. Divine Oneness

The New Testament gives two legitimate ways to express divine oneness. The first way may be summarized as follows: the Father is the one true God. There is a great deal of New Testament evidence in this regard. For example, Jesus referred to the Father as the "only true God" (John 17:3). Jesus' belief in Father God is clearly seen in several other passages: on the cross Jesus referred to the Father as "My God" (Matt., 27:46; Mark 15:34), and after his resurrection he said to Mary, "Stop clinging to Me, for I have not yet ascended to the Father; but go to My brethren, and say to them, 'I ascend to My Father and your Father, and My God and your God'" (John 20:17). From these passages we get Jesus' understanding of God in a nutshell: he believes that there is only one true God, that the one true God is the Father, and that Father God is his God and the God of his followers. Anything else Jesus said about God, or about himself for that matter, must be understood in this light. Significantly, Paul the theologian was equally clear on this expression divine oneness. For him there is "one God, the Father, from whom all things came and for whom we live" (1 Cor. 8:6, NIV; cf. Rom. 16:27; Eph. 4:6; 1 Tim. 2:5).

I believe that this New Testament way of expressing divine oneness addresses the monotheism question. By identifying the one true God as the Father, there is clear and straightforward continuity between both Testaments: the "Lord is one" of the Shema is the "only true God" of Jesus and the "one God" of Paul. For both Jesus and Paul, the monotheism of the old dispensation is extended into the new, but now with a greater emphasis on God as Father.

The second New Testament way of expressing divine oneness does not address the monotheism question per se, but it is important just the same. This divine oneness concerns the relationship between the persons of the trinity. John's Gospel, perhaps more than any other New Testament book, discusses the nature of this relationship. John described the close and intimate communion between the Father and the Son in vivid terms, reaching its apex in the following words of Jesus: "the Father is in Me, and I in the Father" (10:38; cf. 14:11). Surprisingly, Jesus did not limit this unique wording to the trinity proper, for he used it again to describe his desire for all believers, that they may be one as the Father and the Son are one:

> "I do not ask in behalf of these alone, but for those also who believe in Me through their word; that they may all be one; even as Thou, Father, art in Me, and I in Thee, that they also may be in Us; that the world may believe that Thou didst send Me. And the glory which Thou hast given Me I have given to them; that they may be one, just as We are one; I in them, and Thou in Me, that they may be perfected in unity, that the world may know that Thou didst send Me, and didst love them, even as Thou didst love Me" (John 17:20–23).

Now, I would like to pause for some reflection on what has been said thus far in order to show that both New Testament ways to express divine oneness are in harmony with and illumined by the ontological order. Let's start with the first New Testament way to express divine oneness and ask ourselves the following question: why is the Father the one true God? Or, stated a bit differently, what is it that sets the Father apart from everyone else and defines him as God? First off, it is safe to assume that it is not something that the persons of the trinity have in common. This eliminates *personality* from the list of possibilities, for they each have identical personalities. We will have to look elsewhere for the Father's uniqueness.

So, what is it that sets the Father apart from everyone else and defines him as God? What can be said about the Father that cannot be said about the Son or the Spirit? I believe that the ontological order provides a workable solution here. The Father's uniqueness may be understood as follows: the Father is unique as Originator and head of the ontological order; and as such, he is the source of all things, the fountain of life and wisdom, and the chief architect who oversees everything that takes place in creation. It is this uniqueness that sets the Father apart and defines him as God: God is the Originator and head of the ontological order; the Originator and head of the ontological order is God.

But, then, what about divine works? How do they relate to this definition of God? With what we have already established thus far, that God is the Originator and head of the ontological order, we can now link the Father to divine works and to the divine labels associated with them. Father God is the Originator and head of the ontological order, and as such, he is the source and chief architect of all divine works. Here, divine works are uniquely *his* works. This step allows us to take the next and aptly acknowledge the Father for his participation in divine works. The Father's primal role in divine works establishes him as the rightful owner of all divine labels based on divine works, including Creator, Sustainer, Savior, and the source of prophetic utterance.

Of course, this raises the obvious question: if the Father is the sole owner of such labels, how can we account for the fact that they may be applied to the Son? This question will be addressed in the next subsection.

As noted earlier, the second New Testament way to express divine oneness does not address the monotheism question per se. It has to do with corporate oneness, a oneness centered on the relationship between the persons of the trinity. In this regard, the ontological order can help to clarify the nature of this ongoing and dynamic relationship, adding additional content to the claim of Jesus, that the Father is in him, and he is in the Father. According to the ontological order, the Father and the Son are united by the Spirit, and by the Spirit they commune with one another in the most intimate fashion possible. Within the confines of this relationship, they give themselves to one another in an exchange of thoughts and feelings expressed in an atmosphere of willing cooperation, mutual respect, and self-giving love. This, I believe, provides an appropriate context for the second expression of divine oneness: It is close and intimate communion between the Father and the Son *by the Spirit*. Thus the essence of corporate oneness is, perhaps more than anything else, a Spirit-led community, expressing itself as one heart and one mind through one purpose.

Also, as noted earlier, the second New Testament

way of expressing divine oneness is not exclusive. While the trinity proper does not change, it nevertheless allows others to join in and share in this oneness. At spiritual rebirth a believer is indwelt by the person of the Holy Spirit. The indwelling presence of the Spirit weds the believer to the triune community; and, as an adopted son or daughter with full privileges, he or she may participate in the fellowship between the persons of the trinity.

3. Divine Presence

In the previous subsection, I defined Jewish monotheism as follows: the Father is the one true God. I also showed that this is in harmony with the New Testament witness and the ontological order. It is now time to ask several difficult questions. What about passages that refer to Jesus with divine names, such as God or the exalted use of Lord? The passages that ascribe worship to him also present a problem. How do we interpret them in light of the Old Testament command to worship the one true God alone (e.g., Deut. 6:13–15)? Once again, I believe that the ontological order provides a reasonable answer to these questions. Here we will see both New Testament ways to express divine oneness cross paths, where Father God is made visible through the dynamics of the triune community.

In keeping with the ontological order, the one true God, the Father, operates through the Son and by the Spirit. As discussed earlier, this pattern of operation is consistent with all divine works. This pattern can also help us better understand how God manifests his presence. Let's begin with the Old Testament witness.

In the Old Testament, God manifested his presence

in something or someone else. For example, a "firepot" (Gen. 15:17, NIV), a pillar of smoke and a pillar of fire (Exod. 13:21), and the temple (2 Chron. 7:1–2) are several things in which God manifested his presence. Perhaps the best examples are the humanlike figures who make a brief appearance in the Old Testament. Included here are the angel of the Lord, the angel who appeared to Moses in the burning bush, and the figure who stood before Joshua and identified himself as the "captain of the host of the Lord." Assuming that these figures were actual angels of some kind, we may conclude that they were not God, but figures who effectively manifested the presence of God, so much so that they spoke as God and they were referred to with divine names.[23] Put another way, God so overshadowed these figures that those who looked upon them were able to see God.

Assuming the pattern of the ontological order as a given, we can surmise the Son's role during the Old Testament period. The Son, though invisible and unknown, served to mediate the Father's presence, a presence that was then manifested in something or someone else.

In the New Testament, we do not see God manifesting his presence in, for example, a pillar of fire or the angel of the Lord. Instead, we see God manifest his presence directly in his incarnate Son. Consider the incident where Philip asked Jesus to show them (the disciples) the Father. Jesus responded with the following words, "He who has seen Me has seen the Father. . . . Do you not believe that I am in the Father, and the Father is in Me? The Words that I say to you I do not speak on my own initiative, but the Father abiding in Me does his work" (John 14:9–10). Paul expressed the same idea this way: "For God [the Father] was pleased to have all his fullness dwell in him [Christ], and through him to reconcile to himself all things" (Col. 1:19, NIV; cf. 2:9). From these passages we may conclude several things: (1) The Father was in his Son doing his work, and (2) this reality as Jesus understood it was visible to his followers.

Unlike as in times past, the Son's new role is direct and observable. While maintaining his place and function in the ontological order, the Son, now bodily present, manifests the Father's presence in himself. In this case, mediation (the means to the end) and manifestation (the end itself) overlap and become somewhat interrelated ideas. The expression *through his Son* now encompasses the expression *in his Son*.

The ontological order provides several additional insights into the Son's role that will prove helpful. First, the Old Testament ways in which God manifested his presence were limited, merely foreshadowing what was to come. The Son, on the other hand, is the archetype of all earlier types. As Mediator, he is perfectly suited to manifest the fullness of the Father's presence; he has full and intimate access to the Father, and as a divine person, he is fully capable of mirroring the Father's character.

Second, the Son's role is highly personal in nature, centering primarily in the will. The Son perfectly manifests the Father's presence because he perfectly submits himself in love and thus becomes an ideal vessel for another. To be sure, there is a metaphysical angle to all this, in which the Spirit plays an integral role in the process. By the Spirit the Father leads, and by the Spirit the Son joyfully follows. Nonetheless, the key to mediation is in the Son's self-giving and obedient attitude. In the words of Jesus, "Truly, truly, I say to you, the Son can do nothing on Himself, unless it is something He sees the Father doing; for whatever the Father does, these things the Son also does in like manner" (John 5:19).

Having said this about the Father abiding in the Son and doing his work, let's look at the other key idea stated earlier: according to Jesus, the Father's presence in him was visible to his followers. Of course, Jesus' words are somewhat enigmatic; though the Father's presence in the Son is visible, it is not visible to all. It is only visible to those with ears to hear and eyes to see, i.e., to those with spiritual discernment. The Spirit enables the believer to look at Jesus and see God, both God present and God at work.

This, I believe, is the fundamental reason why divine names were ascribed to Jesus. Those who saw the Father in the Son—either by direct observation or upon later reflection—saw God. As the New Testament writers expressed this reality in written form, they sometimes did so by labeling the vessel with the contents in the vessel, where the identification of Christ as God is an expression of the revelation of God in Christ. Thus his divine names do not speak of his personal deity, but of deity in his person. They are a compact way of saying that he embodies the one true God; that in him God is present, active, and visible; that in him God is approachable, accessible, and available; and that in him God is most accurately understood and most intimately known.

The Father's other divine labels, which stem from his identity as Originator, such as Creator, Sustainer, Savior, and the source of prophetic utterance, are attached to Christ in a similar fashion. As the Son mediates divine works, and he is recognized as the focal point of the Father's presence, purpose, and power in doing so, he takes on the Father's labels associated with those works.

From here we can see how worship could be ascribed to Jesus. With the dawning of the first century, the one true God, the Father, remained the sole object of worship (e.g., John 4:23; Eph. 3:14). In this respect things had not changed. The monotheism of the Old Testament was still in force. However, what had changed was *how* God revealed himself. Father God was now visible in Jesus Christ. Some in the first century who had an open mind and a receptive heart discerned this fact. During times of illumination, Jesus became a window revealing the fullness of God—God's power, God's love, God's wisdom, God's compassion, etc. Jesus himself was a living tabernacle with the flap pulled back, allowing everyone to look in. Those who recognized what they were looking at, even if only for a moment and with partial understanding, often responded in worship. The basic pattern of Christian worship is seen here: God is worshiped through the Son and by the Spirit.

Of course, this theory must be applied with discretion. Not all divine names ascribed to Jesus should be understood exactly the same, and likewise with worship. Context should help to sort such things out. Nonetheless, from a theological perspective, this theory provides a plausible explanation for how the early Jewish disciples could maintain their belief in one God and, at the same time, refer to Jesus with divine names and offer him worship.

F. Summary

This chapter developed the following understanding of the trinity: the trinity consists of three persons, namely the Father, the Son, and the Holy Spirit. They are in a fixed and eternal arrangement, referred to as the ontological order. This arrangement governs their relationship with one another and with creation. It embraces personal as well as corporate distinctives. In a personal sense, the Father, the Son, and the Holy Spirit each operate according to the full perfection of divine personality. In a corporate sense, they share in a relationship characterized by intimacy, order, diversity, and harmony.

In regard to omnipresence before the incarnation and after the resurrection, the Father and the Son are located in heaven (which is somewhere in the spiritual realm), while the person of the Holy Spirit permeates the whole of creation (or both realms). In regard to imminence, the Holy Spirit serves as the Father and the Son's spiritual "senses," the means by which they observe and participate in the affairs of everyday life. In this way the Spirit provides them with all present information about both realms. In regard to monotheism, the Father as Originator and head of the ontological order is the one true God. The Son perfectly manifested the Father's presence on earth; and this manifestation was the basis for the Son's divine identity.

This understanding of the trinity will serve as the foundation for further theological development. In the next chapter, a theory of the incarnate Christ will be "assembled" upon this trinitarian "chassis" to complete the proposed theological system.

Notes

1. For this study, time, space, and matter come into existence at the same moment. This is difficult to prove from Scripture alone; however, several passages seem to indicate that this is so. For example, Hebrews 1:2 is sometimes interpreted as a reference to the creation of the universe of space and time (F. F. Bruce, *The Epistle to the Hebrews,* revised edition, The New International Commentary on the New Testament [Grand Rapids: Eerdmans

Publishing Co., 1990], p. 47). Other passages such as Genesis 1:1 and John 1:1 seem to indicate a similar idea.
2. For the sake of simplicity, the physical realm and spiritual realm come into existence at the same time (represented by a single vertical line labeled *Beginning*). This may or may not be the case. The Bible is silent on this issue. On the one hand, the origination time of each realm may differ from one another without impacting the point of the illustration. A difference of this kind would simply make the illustration more complex. On the other hand, the idea that both realms did have a beginning is much more significant. To propose that a realm has always existed would make it eternal, a position which I believe incorrectly ascribes to creation that which should only be said about the persons of the trinity.
3. The name *Eternal Father* does not mean that the Son, the second person of the trinity, and the Father, the first person of the trinity, are one and the same. According to one author, this title may merely be a way of designating the Messiah "not only as the possessor of eternity, but as the tender, faithful, and wise trainer, guardian, and provider for His people even in eternity" (C. F. Keil and F. Delitzsch, vol. 7, *Commentary on the Old Testament* [Massachusetts: Hendrickson Publishers, 1986], Isaiah 1:27, p. 253).
4. E. J. Fortman, *The Triune God* (London: Hutchinson, 1972), p. 5.
5. W. E. Elwell, ed., *Evangelical Dictionary of Theology* (Grand Rapids: Baker Book House, 1984), p. 727.
6. Most scholars believe that verse 8 is a later addition to the text.
7. Keep in mind that this discussion is limited in scope. I have selected those aspects of personality which are necessary for future theological development.
8. Old Testament references to God are generally attributed to the Father. With this in mind, the following emotions may be included: anger (Job 19:11; Lam. 2:1–3; Ezek. 5:13; Zeph. 3:8), compassion (Deut. 32:36; Ps. 111:4), grief (Gen. 6:6), hate (Ps. 5:5; 11:5), jealousy (Exod. 20:5), joy (Ps. 104:31; Isa. 62:5), love (Jer. 31:3), and mercy (Neh. 9:31).
9. The Greek word for like substance is *homoiousia,* while the word for same substance is *homoousia.* The difference between these two Greek words is only one letter; however, the difference each word makes in regard to Christology is very significant. The former word makes Jesus less than God, while the latter regards him as God.
10. P. Schaff, *The Creeds of Christendom,* vol. 1 (Grand Rapids: Baker Book House, 1993), p. 29.

11. Ibid.
12. Scholars typically define eternity in one of two ways. Some view eternity as everlastingness (or God's existence for all time), while others view eternity as timelessness (or God's existence outside of time). Which view is right? This is a difficult question to answer. Both views of eternity have been adopted by great Christian theologians and church leaders throughout the years. I am of the opinion that both understandings of eternity—God exists for all time and, in some sense, outside of time—are legitimate; but that the Bible highly favors the former interpretation over the latter. An excellent discussion can be found in R. H. Nash's *The Concept of God* (Grand Rapids: Zondervan Publishing House, 1983), pp. 73–83.
13. The begetting of the Son described here is similar to the concept of eternal generation. For a brief description of eternal generation, see L. Berkhof, *Systematic Theology* (Grand Rapids: Eerdmans Publishing Co., 1941), pp. 93–94.
14. Keep in mind that the word *origin* is used simply to express the idea that the Son has his origin in someone else. It should not be confused with the word *beginning*. This word is a time-relative word, a word which assumes a time when something was not but now is.
15. Ontology is the branch of metaphysics dealing with the nature of being or reality.
16. S. Charnock, *The Existence and Attributes of God,* vol. 1 (Grand Rapids: Baker Book House, 1979), p. 374.
17. H. Bavinck, *The Doctrine of God* (Edinburgh: Banner of Truth, 1977), p. 162.
18. Ibid.
19. Ibid., p. 163.
20. Several passages appear to say that the Son is omnipresent. For example, Matthew 18:20 records these words of Jesus, "For where two or three have gathered together in My name, there I am in their midst" (cf. Matt. 28:20; Eph. 1:23; 3:17; Col. 3:11). In light of the argument presented, this passage simply means that the Son is present by way of the Spirit, who provides him immediate and intimate access everywhere in creation.
21. A brief but excellent historical account which traces the formulation of the doctrine of the trinity may be found in E. C. Beisner's *God in Three Persons* (Wheaton, Illinois: Tyndale House Publishers, 1978).
22. G. R. Lewis and B. A. Demarest, *Integrative Theology,* vol. 1 (Grand Rapids: Zondervan Publishing House, 1987), p. 255. Substance and essence are interchangeable terms.

23. I am developing my argument assuming that these figures were actual angels of some kind, for I believe that this is the most likely option. But it is possible that, as some Christian scholars claim, these Old Testament figures were early appearances of the preincarnate Christ in a temporal humanlike form. It is important to note that this option does not present an insurmountable obstacle for the proposed system. The key here is to recognize that such appearances are a close parallel to the incarnation. Thus, while allowing for the obvious differences between a spiritual form and a physical form, Old Testament appearances of the preincarnate Christ could be handled in much the same way as the New Testament appearance of the incarnate Christ, where, as we shall soon see, God manifested his presence in his Son.

III. The Person of Christ

"He said to him the third time, 'Simon, son of John, do you love Me?' Peter was grieved because He said to him the third time, 'Do you love Me?' And he said to Him, 'Lord, You know all things; You know that I love You' " (John 21:17). Peter failed Jesus when the going got tough. But he did not fail to learn at least one important thing about his Lord: Jesus possessed extensive knowledge, knowledge detailed enough to include his innermost thoughts and feelings. Peter's confession is understandable in light of the Gospel accounts, for they ascribe extraordinary knowledge to Jesus Christ. This is the positive side of things, however. Not all the New Testament witness is so favorable. This chapter will begin by giving the "big picture" perspective concerning the incarnate Christ's knowledge. A survey of what Jesus did and perhaps did not know will prove illuminating. Later in this investigation, these passages will be used for evaluating the proposed theological system.

Jesus knew who he was. He identified himself as the Son of God (Luke 22:70), the Son of Man (John 8:28), and the Messiah (4:25–26). He also revealed his identity through titles, such as the bread of life (6:35), the light of the world (8:12), the good shepherd (10:14), and the way, and the truth, and the life (14:6). He claimed to be the eternal *I Am* who existed before Abraham was born (8:58). Jesus publicly proclaimed that he was the "anointed One" who came to set the captives free (Luke 4:17–21), as foretold by the prophet Isaiah (Isa. 61:1–2). In addition to self-knowledge, he claimed intimate knowledge of the Father (John 7:29; 10:15; 15:1) and the Spirit (16:5–15).

Jesus knew Scripture. At the age of twelve, Jesus' knowledge and understanding of the Law amazed some religious leaders (Luke 2:47). He would later use Scripture against Satan in the wilderness (Matt. 4:1–11). He understood Scripture in regard to cleansing (Matt. 8:4; Mark 1:44; Luke 5:14) and divorce (Matt. 19:3–9; Mark 10:2–9). He also displayed his knowledge of the Ten Commandments to a rich young ruler (Matt. 19:18–19; Mark 10:19; Luke 18:20). While walking with several disciples on the road to Emmaus, he "explained to them the things concerning Himself in all the Scriptures" (Luke 24:27). John noted that his teaching was a marvel to many (John 7:15).

Jesus knew the physical world. He often explained spiritual truth using illustrations drawn from everyday life (e.g., Matt. 18:12–14; Luke 14:28–30). He also knew where things could be found. He knew where to let down the nets to catch many fish (Luke 5:4) as well as the location of a particular fish with a coin in its mouth (Matt. 17:27). He knew where to find a colt (Matt. 21:2; Mark 11:2; Luke 19:30), where to find a guest room for the Passover meal (Mark 14:13–15; Luke 22:10–13), and where Nathanael had been (John 1:48). Jesus knew much about the world around him, and, as several of these examples show, his knowledge went beyond that which could be gained by natural senses alone.

Jesus knew humanity. John wrote, "But Jesus, on His part, was not entrusting Himself to them, for He knew all men, and because He did not need anyone to bear witness concerning man for He Himself knew what was in man" (John 2:24–25). He knew the nature and operation of sin (Matt. 15:11; Mark 7:15; John 8:34). He knew those who followed him for personal gain (John 6:26) as well as the hypocrisy of the religious leaders (Matt. 23:1–7; 16–36; Mark 12:38–40; Luke 20:45–47). He knew Nathanael's true character (John 1:47–48), an assessment he made from a distance. And, as Scripture records many times, Jesus knew the very thoughts of others (e.g., Matt. 9:4; 12:25; Mark 2:8; 8:17; Luke 5:22; 6:8; 9:47; 11:17).

Jesus knew the spiritual world. A primary focus of his ministry was to proclaim the good news of the kingdom of heaven (Matt. 4:23; 9:35). To the disciples he revealed the mysteries of the kingdom in parables. He likened the kingdom to a mustard seed, yeast, hidden treasure, and a net. He explained how one may enter the kingdom as well as the fate of those who chose to remain outside. He also understood the nature of the kingdom of darkness. He warned the disciples that Satan and his cohorts would oppose the work of God (Mark 4:15). He was keenly aware of demonic activity around him and frequently exorcised a demon(s) with a word. Jesus knew a great deal about the nature and activity of the unseen spiritual realm.

Jesus knew historical events. He mentioned that Moses had allowed divorce because of the hard hearts of the people (Matt. 19:8; Mark 10:5) and that David and his men ate the consecrated bread (Luke 6:3–4). Jesus also mentioned a historical event not found in Old Testament Scripture; he used the collapse of a tower to explain a spiritual truth (13:4). He knew about historical events in the recent past, often without direct access to such information. For example, he knew the woman at the well had five previous husbands (John 4:18). In fact, she later said to the people of the town, "Come, see a man who told me all the things that I have done; this is not the Christ, is it?" (4:29). He also knew that the man at the pool had been there a long time (5:6) and that Lazarus had already died (11:14). Jesus had a comprehensive, factual knowledge of the past.

Jesus knew details about the future in regard to his mission. He knew his mission was to save the lost (Luke 19:10; John 12:47). But he also knew his mission would not bring peace but a sword (Matt. 10:34). He knew he would be rejected by the people and deserted by his disciples (Matt. 26:31; Mark 14:27). He even knew which disciple would betray him (Matt. 26:21–25; John 13:26). He knew that he would face tremendous suffering and death by crucifixion (Matt. 20:19; 26:2). But he also knew that he would rise from the dead on the third day (Matt. 17:9, 23; 20:19; Mark 9:31; 10:34; Luke 18:33), ascend into heaven (John 14:28; 16:10), and someday return to earth with a host of angels to reward the faithful (Matt. 16:27).

Jesus knew of other future events. He warned the disciples of the coming persecution (Matt. 10:21–23), as well as the imminent destruction of the temple (Matt. 24:2; Mark 13:2; Luke 21:6) and Jerusalem (Luke 19:43–44). He informed Peter that he would deny him three times (Luke 22:34; John 13:38). He knew much about the punishment awaiting the wicked (Luke 12:2–5) and the rewards in store for the faithful (14:14). He talked about the end times at great length. He taught about the natural disasters that will take place, the many false Christs who would come, and the universal proclamation of the gospel, which will proceed the end (Matt. 24). He also explained the nature and certainty of the future resurrection (Matt. 22:30; Mark 12:25; Luke

20:35-36). Much of the future was known by the prophet from Nazareth.

As this short survey has shown, the Gospel accounts ascribe extraordinary knowledge to Jesus Christ. However, this is not the whole story. Other New Testament passages seem to indicate that his knowledge was limited. For example, Luke records that he increased in wisdom (Luke 2:40, 52). Jesus also asked many questions. Amidst a large crowd, he asked the disciples who touched him (Mark 5:30; Luke 8:45). He asked a father how long his son had been demon-possessed (Mark 9:21), the disciples how many loaves of bread they had (Matt. 15:34), and those weeping where they had laid the lifeless body of Lazarus (John 11:34). Mark records an incident that seems to indicate that Jesus lacked knowledge. Leaving Bethany, he walked up to a fig tree to see if it had fruit on it (Mark 11:12-14).

Several other passages appear to indicate that Jesus lacked knowledge about the future. He advised the people to pray that their flight may not be in the winter or on a Sabbath (Matt. 24:20; Mark 13:18). He himself prayed that Simon's faith would not fail him (Luke 22:32). It is difficult to imagine why Jesus would offer such advice or pray such a prayer if he already knew in advance what would take place!

One passage forcefully asserts that Jesus lacked knowledge about the future. In regard to his second coming, he said, "But of that day and hour no one knows, not even the angels of heaven, *nor the Son,* but the Father alone" (Matt. 24:36, italics added; cf. Mark 13:32). The fact that these words come from Jesus himself are a testimony to his open honesty and genuine humility.

The biblical evidence presents a difficult challenge for the theologian. To develop a theory of the person of

Christ that accounts for his vast yet limited knowledge is no small undertaking. It is, nevertheless, the goal of this chapter to complete the theological system in order to provide just such a theory.

A. A Complex Figure

"Jesus answered them, 'I showed you many good works from the Father; for which of them are you stoning Me?' The Jews answered Him, 'For a good work we do not stone You, but for blasphemy; and because You, being a man, make Yourself out to be God' " (John 10:32–33). Many in the first century found it hard to believe that the child of Joseph and Mary could be all that he claimed to be. What made this even more difficult to comprehend was that his startling identity and mission were not publicly revealed until he was about thirty years old. Like an unexpected flash flood in the desert, the Messiah arrived on the scene and upset the religious order of the day.

Despite the difficulty for many in the first century to believe the true identity of Jesus, those who knew him well affirmed that he was indeed a unique individual. The New Testament writers claimed two basic truths about Jesus. First, they affirmed that he was a man (e.g., Matt. 8:27; Acts 2:22; 17:31; Rom. 5:17, 19; 1 Cor. 15:21, 47; Phil. 2:8; 1 Tim. 2:5).[1] He had a physical body of flesh and blood (Heb. 2:14), a body that underwent normal human development from conception to adulthood. Luke recorded that he "continued to grow and become strong, increasing in wisdom; and the grace of God was upon Him" (Luke 2:40). Like other human beings, he experienced the passions of life (e.g., Matt. 9:36; 14:14; Mark 3:5; 8:2; 14:33; John 11:35). He was subject to hunger (Matt. 4:2;

21:18), thirst (John 19:28), aging (Luke 2:24; 3:23), fatigue (Mark 4:38; John 4:6), and even death (John 19:30; Phil. 2:8). Judging by outward appearance, he resembled all other men.

Second, the New Testament writers affirmed that Jesus was more than a man. He was conceived in a supernatural way; the Holy Spirit came upon a virgin to produce a unique child (Luke 1:35). To John, the incarnation meant the "Word became flesh, and dwelt among us" (John 1:14). To Paul, the Son "existed in the form of God ... but emptied Himself, taking the form of a bond-servant, and being made in the likeness of men" (Phil. 2:6–7). Unlike all other human beings, Jesus existed before conception. He was a pre-existent being who willfully chose to leave his heavenly glory and live among us. His entrance onto the human stage was a unique event in world history, setting the stage for a truly remarkable life. Clearly, the biblical writers revealed a Jesus who stood out and stood above his peers.

The New Testament writers taught that Jesus was a man, yet a man unlike any other man. He is a complex figure who defies a simple explanation. This chapter is where the rubber meets the road, where I take on the formidable task of defining the person of Christ. As a means to this end, I will "assemble" a one-nature theory of the incarnate Christ on the trinitarian "chassis" developed in chapter 2. After "assembly" is complete, this theory will be evaluated based on its interpretation of the biblical passages concerning Christ's knowledge presented at the beginning of this chapter. But before beginning, I would like to discuss a common interpretation of the two-nature theory and how it accounts for Christ's knowledge. This theory will prove useful later in this study.

B. Two-Nature Theory

How was Jesus both God and man? This question dominated religious thought for the first four and a half centuries of the church. A great deal of time was spent sifting through options to find an acceptable solution. By the fourth century, the commonly held view was that the incarnate Christ had two natures, one human and the other divine. Against the tide of popular opinion, an elderly monk named Eutyches (d. 454) proposed an alternative theory. He insisted that divinity and humanity united at the incarnation to form one nature. In the eyes of many, this theory was unbalanced and deficient, failing to maintain the distinct identity of each nature.

In the West, Pope Leo I (d. 461) opposed the efforts of Eutyches. He wrote a theological treaty, called the *Tome,* condemning his position. In the East, church bishops called a council at Ephesus in 449 to discuss the matter. At Ephesus, the majority was decidedly sympathetic to the position of Eutyches. Leo reacted abruptly to the decision of the council, calling it a "robber synod." Favoring Leo's position, Emperor Marcion summoned a council at Chalcedon in A.D. 451 to resolve the matter.

At the Council of Chalcedon, more than five hundred bishops met to discuss Christological issues. In the end, the council deemed the position of Eutyches heretical. Most present were content to ratify the Nicene tradition, letters of Cyril of Alexandria to Nestorius and John of Antioch, and Leo's *Tome.*[2] To the dismay of many, the emperor insisted that a confession of faith was essential to maintain the unity of the empire. After much deliberation, the council produced a statement known as the Chalcedonian Creed.

The Chalcedonian Creed affirmed that Christ is both

"truly God and truly man."[3] It goes on to state that he is one person consisting of two natures, one human and the other divine. He is "to be acknowledged in two natures, inconfusedly, unchangeably, indivisibly, inseparably; the distinction of natures being by no means taken away by the union, but rather the property of each nature being preserved, and concurring in one Person and one Subsistence, not parted or divided into two persons, but one and the same Son."[4] In Mary's womb, the preexistent Son (with a divine nature) united with humanity (a human nature and a physical body) to become the God-man.

The emperor had hoped that a formal confession would unify the empire. To his dismay, the immediate result of the council was a split within the Eastern Church. The Coptic churches in Egypt and Ethiopia did not accept the decision of the council, holding to a particular one nature theory called monophysitism. Repeated attempts to resolve the conflict within the Eastern Church were unsuccessful. Nevertheless, from this time forward, and despite harsh criticism from time to time, the Chalcedonian statement would serve as a foundational creed and the standard of orthodoxy in the West as well as much of the East for the next fifteen hundred plus years.

In summary, the two-nature theory views the incarnate Christ as one person with two natures, one human and the other divine, each nature with its own conscience, will, and attributes.[5] The natures share in an eternal union without confusion, without change, without division, and without separation. "These phrases represent an apophotic theology (a negative theology stating what is not) as a way of affirming the paradox that the two natures are present in the one person."[6] This negative approach does not—nor was it intended to—remove the mystery of the union; but it "simply seeks to safeguard the truth against various heretical views."[7]

For the most part, the Chalcedonian statement is accepted and taught in most conservative circles. Theologically speaking, the incarnate Christ is a single person with two natures, one human and the other divine, each nature with its own conscious, will, and attributes. Functionally speaking, Christ may operate in accord with his human nature one moment and in accord with his divine nature the next. Although his natures have distinct spheres of operation, Christ has the ability to control what each nature will do and when it will do it, and he ensures that they always operate in harmony with one another. The operation of either nature is always attributed to the same person: Jesus Christ.

The natural corollary to this theory is the following hermeneutic. Biblical passages that show Jesus display weakness are attributed to his human nature, while passages that show him display supernatural qualities are attributed to his divine nature. Thus the incarnate Christ encompasses seemingly contradictory things—he is short on knowledge yet omniscient, limited in power yet omnipotent, localized in presence yet omnipresent, lacking in wisdom yet possessing the wisdom of God, and so forth. With this in mind, it is time for this theological system to produce a "product." This understanding of the two-nature theory will now interpret the biblical passages concerning the incarnate Christ's knowledge given earlier in this chapter.

As a man, the incarnate Christ had limited knowledge, which increased with the passing of time. In other words, he grew in knowledge with respect to his human nature. Passages that show him display weakness appear to support this claim. For example, he increased in wisdom and displayed ignorance on several occasions. He asked where Lazarus' body was laid. He was uncertain if a fig tree had fruit on it. He also admitted he did not know the time of the end. It is important to note that these passages relate to Christ's human nature alone; during times of ignorance, he chose not to operate within the sphere of his divine nature, which possessed all knowledge.

As God, the incarnate Christ was omniscient. In other words, he possessed all knowledge (past, present, and future) with respect to his divine nature. Passages that show Christ display supernatural knowledge appear to support this claim. For example, Jesus knew where to let down the nets to catch many fish as well as the location of a particular fish with a coin in its mouth. He knew Nathanael's character before they met, that the woman at the well had five previous husbands, that Lazarus had already died, and that Peter would deny him three times. He also knew the thoughts of others. Additional support for omniscience is seen in the comment made by the disciples (John 16:30) and later Peter (21:17), that Jesus knew "all things."

I will not discuss the "quality" of this "product" now, but address this matter in my closing comments. It is worth mentioning that, while I have offered a common interpretation of the two-nature theory, it is not the only interpretation. Among other things, not all theologians agree on how Christ's natures relate to one another, and how they relate to his knowledge. With this in mind, the reader is advised to consult several theological volumes that discuss the two-nature theory in detail in order to gain a fuller understanding of this particular doctrine.[8]

C. One-Nature Theory

Throughout church history numerous attempts have been made to develop a one-nature theory of the incarnate Christ. Some early efforts in the fourth century were labeled Word-flesh Christologies. Word-flesh Christologies existed in different forms. In general, they espoused the idea that the eternal Word overshadowed or replaced all or part of Christ's human nature and served as the operational center of his inner life. Advocates such as Apollinarius (d. 391) argued unsuccessfully for their position.[9]

Apollinarius' Word-flesh Christology and the proposed solution are both one-nature theories. Their commonality may lead some to believe that they have identical weaknesses and should be rejected for the same reasons. Such an approach oversimplifies things. The criticism lodged against Apollinarius should be discriminatingly applied to the proposed solution, for while both systems may appear to be saying the same thing, they are substantiated in very different ways, resting upon completely different world views and presuppositions. But, then again, the criticism against Apollinarius is not without value. It provides legitimate points of concern, which should be taken seriously.

Millard Erickson notes four major objections to Apollinarius' Word-flesh Christology: (1) His theory was docetic, in that Jesus only appeared like a man, (2) because Jesus did not have a human psychology, he was not strictly human, but some strange monstrosity, (3) the absence of a human psychology seemed to conflict with the Gospel's description of Jesus, most notably his development, ignorance, and emotions, and (4) assuming a whole human nature was essential to his redemptive work.[10]

Let's look at how each objection will be addressed by the proposed one-nature theory.

The first two objections raise a legitimate concern. Was Jesus a man or did he merely appear human? The primary goal of this chapter is to develop a one-nature theory of the incarnate Christ, which encompasses his amazing uniqueness *and* his authentic humanity, a truly extraordinary man fully capable of sharing in the human experience. (It is worth noting that the first two objections may also be said of the two-nature theory. Does not a man with two natures only appear to be a man like other men? Is not a man with two natures some kind of strange monstrosity? Both theories are open to the same criticism because both theories propose something out of the ordinary.)

The third objection is also a valid concern. How does one explain such limitations in the absence of a human psychology? I will answer this question by showing how the proposed theory adequately addresses Jesus' physical limitations, temptations, growth in wisdom, and lack of knowledge.

The fourth objection must be understood in light of fourth-century thought. The Cappadocians and other Greek theologians understood salvation as *deification*. For the purpose of this discussion, it suffices to say that with deification there is a strong association between Christ's person and his work. Specifically, Christ could only save that which he was united to. Or, in other words, he had to unite with complete humanity—both a human nature and physical body—to save complete humanity.[11] In the famous words of Gregory of Nazianzus (d. 389), "For that which He has not assumed He has not healed, but that which is united to His Godhead is also saved."

Much can be said concerning this argument. However, I would like to offer a few general observations. Deification is rooted in the idea that God and man belong to mutually exclusive categories. The Bible, on the other hand, does not give such a one-dimensional view of things. True, God is without equal. But he also created man in his own image, and their commonality opens the door to more *inclusive* possibilities. Concerning Christ's redemptive work, it suffices to say that his identification with humanity and his sinlessness qualified him as an acceptable sacrifice for the sins of the world.

1. Christ's Humanity

John wrote, "And the Word became flesh, and dwelt among us, and we beheld His glory, glory as of the only begotten from the Father, full of grace and truth" (John 1:14). The phrase "became flesh" does not mean that the Word temporarily donned a fleshly costume. Neither does it mean that the Word mutated into a man. Instead, it means that the Word *became* a human being. The Son voluntarily emptied himself to do this (see Phil. 2:6–7). This "self-emptying" did not alter his essential nature, but it brought about a change of existence from an exalted, metaphysical Son to a lowly, enfleshed servant-Son. In this new incarnate state of existence, the Son would *now* and *forever* be identified with corporal humanity.

A human being is a complex being, part immaterial and part material. Scripture describes the immaterial aspect of a human being in several ways. At times, it is described as a composite of soul and spirit (e.g., 1 Thess. 5:23; Heb. 4:12). In this case, there appears to be a distinction between the soul and spirit. At other times, the immaterial aspect is described as either a soul (e.g., Matt.

```
┌─────────────┐                    ┌─────────────┐
│   Human     │   ╱──────────╲     │   Divine    │
│ Personality │  ╱ Similarity ╲    │ Personality │
├─────────────┤ ⟨      &       ⟩   ├─────────────┤
│  Physical   │  ╲ Difference ╱    │  Physical   │
│    Body     │   ╲──────────╱     │    Body     │
└─────────────┘                    └─────────────┘
      Man                            Incarnate Christ
```

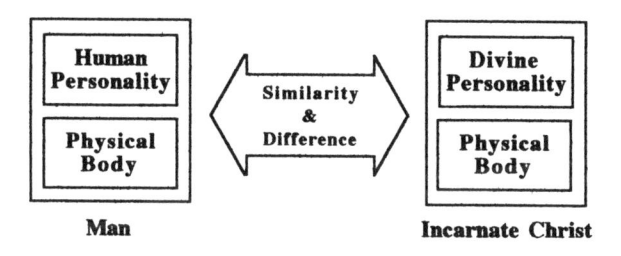

Figure 7: The Incarnate Christ's Likeness to Man

10:28; 16:26) or a spirit (e.g., 1 Cor. 5:5; Luke 23:46). Here, soul and spirit are used as interchangeable words, which refer to the same reality. For this study, rather than choose one view over the other, I will simply refer to the immaterial aspect of a human being as the *inner-man*. The inner-man refers to all that a human being is apart from the *outer-man,* or material body.

For the most part, the biblical writers depict a human being as a unitary being.[12] A human being is identified by the inner-man and outer-man together. Both aspects are present in this life and in the life to come. To be sure, there is a period of separation at death, where the inner-man exists apart from the outer-man. But this is an intermediate state and should be viewed as incomplete or abnormal in light of the reunion which will take place at the coming resurrection.[13] For this reason, Millard Erickson rightly refers to a human being as a "conditional unity."[14]

Figure 7 will serve as a helpful visual aid. Jesus Christ was made in the likeness of man (Rom. 8:3; Phil. 2:7); and, like all men and women, he is a conditional unity of inner-man and outer-man. His inner-man is a divine personality, while his outer-man is a physical body. Let's look at both of these aspects of Christ in more detail.

The Son's divine personality has basic structural elements in common with human personality, including the mind, the will, and the emotions; therefore, it serves as a natural substitute for human personality.[15] It is sufficiently similar to ours to allow him to experience earthly life as we do. But, as discussed earlier, his personality is anything but common; it is uniquely set apart and infinitely superior to our personality.

The incarnation had no adverse effects on his personality. Its functional capabilities were not limited, hindered, or diminished in any way. Thus he continued to express the fullness of divine personality. He was fully conscious of his identity; he exercised complete volitional freedom; he expressed natural and pure emotions; he could participate in any number of relationships simultaneously; and he had unlimited storage capacity and complete real-time access to stored data.

The incarnate Christ has an outer-man, or physical body (e.g., John 2:21; Acts 2:31; Col. 1:22; Heb. 10:5; 1 Peter 2:24; 1 John 4:2; 2 John 7). His body is similar to the body of any other man. It went through the normal stages of human development as he grew to adulthood. There also exists a natural relationship between his inner-man and outer-man; his inner-man received the appropriate input from each of his five senses (hearing, sight, smell, taste, and touch). Whether it be cutting his first teeth, hearing birds sing and roosters crow, smelling freshly baked bread, or observing the spring flowers on a Galilean hillside, Christ experienced life through his natural senses as did his contemporaries—and as we do today.

Figure 8 illustrates the omnipresence of the trinity during the earthly years of the incarnate Christ. The Son moved from the heavenly realm to the physical realm. Despite his change in location, the Son maintained his place

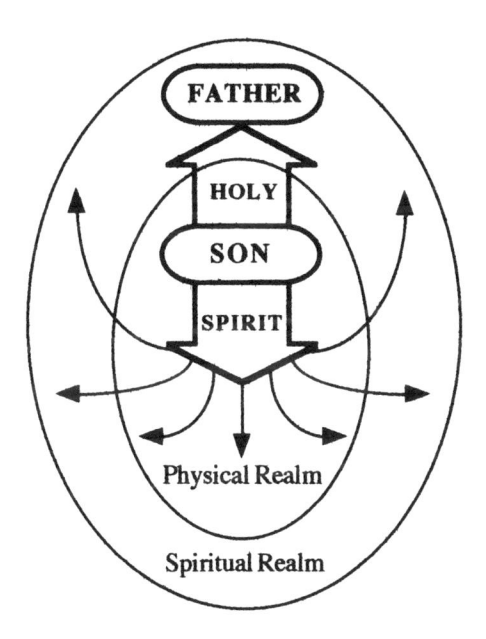

Figure 8: The Omnipresence of the Trinity During the Earthly Years of the Incarnate Christ

and function in the ontological order. During this time the persons of the trinity continued to share in a relationship characterized by intimacy, order, and cooperation. The Son also continued to actively participate in all divine works, such as, for example, sustaining creation.

In accord with the ontological order, the incarnate Christ received a great deal of information directly from his Heavenly Father. Jesus said, "For I did not speak on My own initiative, but the Father Himself who sent Me has given Me commandment, what to say, and what to speak. And I know that His commandment is eternal life; therefore the things I speak, I speak just as the Father has told Me" (John 12:49–50; cf. 7:16; 8:28; 15:15; 17:8).

By the Spirit, the Father and Son continued to freely exchange information just as they had before the incarnation.

He also acquired information about creation in two distinct yet concurrent ways. The first way was through any one of his five senses. Jesus' ears, eyes, nose, tongue, and hands provided him firsthand knowledge of his physical environment. The second way he acquired information was by the Spirit. The Holy Spirit, who was everywhere present in both realms, served as his spiritual "eyes" and "ears." By both natural and supernatural means, Jesus perceived the world around him and gained access to information about creation. Let's discuss his supernatural way of gathering information in a little more detail.

As mentioned earlier, the functional capabilities of his personality were not impacted by the incarnation. Therefore, his supernatural ability to store and gather information continued on throughout his earthy life. The lowly, enfleshed servant-Son retained all past information, and by the Spirit, he acquired all new information in every category the moment when it became available. Consequently, at any given moment in time, Jesus of Nazareth was in full possession of all available information about both realms.

It is important to note that Jesus' ability to gather information was subject to availability. Past and present information was available to him; future information was not. Concerning the latter, the incarnate Christ lacked direct access to future information; therefore, what he did know about tomorrow must have been gained in a roundabout way.

2. Christ's Sinful Flesh

Was Jesus born in sin? Or, more precisely, was he born tainted by sin? The church has traditionally believed that he was born untainted by sin, much like Adam before the Fall (Gen. 3). Some suggest that it was the sanctifying work of the Holy Spirit at conception that produced a holy child untainted by sin (cf. Luke 1:35). Others claim that it is impossible for the Holy Word and "sinful flesh" to coexist together. In the ensuing discussion, the traditional answer will be challenged in light of the biblical evidence and logic.[16] But before giving reasons why I believe the incarnate Christ was tainted by sin, let's first discuss the nature and operation of sin.

Practically speaking, what does "tainted by sin" mean? While it is difficult to put a finger on it, and therefore to produce a dictionary definition of it, if we read between the lines, Scripture does yield insight which allows us to draw the following general conclusions. First, this "tainting" entered creation at the Fall and will exit creation at the end of the age. It is not a necessary part of creation. Second, its presence is felt throughout the entire physical realm. We live in a debased and polluted world, a world in "bondage to decay" (Rom. 8:21, NIV). Third, it functions as a corrupting agent, an invisible contaminant, which brings about organic decay and engenders an inner bias towards sin, serving to heighten and deepen the lure and the grip of sin. Fourth, it is an *it,* not a *he* or *she.* It is not a person, like the Spirit; but closer to a force, like gravity.[17] I prefer to think of it as a principle, a "sin-principle," which is always at work at all places and at all times. Let's dig deeper and continue with how it relates to humanity.

Fifth, the sin-principle infects all human beings.

Paul wrote, "through one man [Adam] sin entered into the world, and death through sin, and so death spread to all men, because all sinned" (Rom. 5:12).[18] Adam's sin introduced the cancer of sin into the human race. As a result, all men and women struggle with sin, some more than others. On an operational level, the sin-principle, in conjunction with human free will, promotes wrong behavior. It contributes to the force of temptation, pressing one to give in and perform a sinful act. In the end, it is the sinful act that is the basis for judgment, and apart from proper atonement leads to condemnation. Thus a human being is sinful by *association* but a sinner by *participation.*

Sixth, the sin-principle affects the whole individual. The outer-man, or material body, is influenced by sin. As mentioned earlier, it makes organic decay possible. Apart from divine intervention, aging and physical death are inescapable. The sin-principle acts upon the inner-man in a different way. Since the inner-man is immaterial, it is not subject to organic decay. Nonetheless, the sin-principle, an invisible intruder within, is bent on destruction. From conception to death, the sin-principle is a relentless force, which seeks to entangle its host, primarily through destructive, habitual patterns of behavior. Those *controlled* by sin cannot live a life pleasing to God (Rom. 8:8). Although, at times, Scripture refers to the enslaved inner-man as *sarx,* translated "flesh" or "sin nature" (NIV; see Rom. 7:18), one must not lose sight of the fact that the inner-man and the sin-principle are distinct entities, the former controlled and held in bondage by the latter.

Finally, the sin-principle will eventually defeat all humanity. Paul was very sure about this. He wrote, "for all have sinned and fall short of the glory of God" (Rom. 3:23). This applies not only to those living before and during Paul's day, but to all future generations as well. In the following words, Paul describes his futile struggle with sin:

> For I know that nothing good dwells in me, that is, in my flesh; for the wishing is present in me, but the doing of the good is not. For the good that I wish, I do not do; but I practice the very evil that I do not wish. But if I am doing the very thing I do not wish, I am no longer the one doing it, but sin which dwells in me. I find then the principle that evil is present in me, the one who wishes to do good. For I joyfully concur with the law of God in the inner man, but I see a different law in the members of my body, waging war against the law of my mind, and making me a prisoner of the law of sin which is in my members (Rom. 7:18–23).

Each individual has been, is, or will be given the opportunity to wrestle this ominous foe. However, as history has shown time and time again, the sin-principle will emerge victorious in each and every bout.

With this picture of the sin-principle in mind, the following reasons are why I believe that Christ was born tainted by sin.

The sin-principle infected and affected Jesus' whole being. As a real flesh-and-blood man, born at a particular place and a particular time, he fully identified with humanity in the current age, accepting life as it now exists.[19] Like us, his outer-man suffered pain, hunger, thirst, fatigue, aging, and even death. These effects or symptoms are the aftermath of the Fall, evidence that the sin-principle is both present and active. Also like us, Jesus' inner-man was acted upon by the sin-principle. His ordeal in the garden is a graphic example of the same type of inner struggle described by Paul in Romans

7:18–23. Inside Jesus there was a "different law" in the members of his body, waging war against the law of his mind. The presence of the sin-principle contributes to the intensity and direction of this inner struggle, a struggle in which Jesus engages and overcomes through persistent prayer.

The sin-principle was necessary for Jesus to sympathize with human weakness. The author of Hebrews wrote: "For we do not have a high priest who cannot sympathize with our weaknesses, but one who has been tempted in all things as we are, yet without sin" (Heb. 4:15). This passage states that Jesus can sympathize with us because he was tempted like us. Naturally, this assumes that his condition was also like ours, for condition and temptation are bound together, the former a prerequisite of the latter.

We clearly see the relationship between condition and temptation in our case. As suggested earlier, we are not tempted in a "neutral" state. Our sinful condition has an obvious impact on the nature of temptation. The inner bias towards sin makes temptation difficult to resist and overcome. Thus, by applying what is true about humanity in general to Jesus, we can conclude that his sinful flesh *enabled* him to be tempted like us, and as a *result* he became a high priest who can "sympathize with our weaknesses" and help us in our times of need.

By defeating the sin-principle, Jesus achieved a more complete and glorious victory. The position that Jesus was untainted by sin and tempted much like Adam before the Fall detracts from the passion of his struggle and the magnitude of his victory. When the Son came to earth and identified with us, he stepped into the ring to challenge all comers. From time to time, Satan threw a few jabs. The sin-principle, on the other hand, was a relentless attacker. Looking to deliver the knockout blow, it pressured him to transgress God's command at every turn, from the moment of conception to his last words on the cross. Yet, in the end, Jesus successfully resisted all temptation from all opponents; and beyond the cross and the grave, he was crowned champion of all, a victory he won for all of God's creation.

In sum, it was necessary for the incarnate Christ to be born in sin, and thus infected by the sin-principle, to account for his physical trials and inner struggles, to enable him to sympathize with human weakness, and to achieve a more complete and glorious victory. Keep in mind that Christ's sinful condition is limited to his short stay on earth. It does not apply to his post-resurrection existence, in which we see him untainted by sin and thus get a glimpse of life in the age to come.

3. Christ's Vulnerability

At this point several important philosophical questions will be addressed. These questions were raised by the early church theologians, and they have been asked in scholastic circles ever since. The first question goes something like this: How did the incarnate Christ suffer physical trials, aging, and even death? The early church theologians who espoused the two-nature theory provided an answer to this question based on the distinction and the union of Christ's natures. Influenced by the classical idea of perfection taught by men such as Plato and Aristotle, they assumed that God is unaffected by what happens in the world (impassable) and unchanging (immutable); therefore, he is incapable of suffering and death. From here, they concluded that Christ could not suffer physical trials, aging, and death in his divinity, but in his humanity alone. Thomas Oden provides an insightful summary:

> The Savior could suffer, be powerless, and die as a human being, not in his divine nature, but through the possession of humanity. Similarly his soul could feel anguish from the bodily pain, which lacking body it would not feel. So although in his divine nature he was insensible to pain, the God-man was capable through the divine-human union to suffer pain.[20]

To answer this question in light of the proposed one-nature theory, several factors must be considered. The first factor concerns the relationship between the ontological order and power. In accord with the ontological order, power originates with the Father, is mediated through the Son, and is applied by the Spirit to creation. Hence, the Father as Originator is the source of all power. He decides when and how much power is needed to accommodate a given situation; and the Son as Mediator and the Spirit as Applicator follow his lead. In this way all three persons of the trinity participate in creative acts, sustaining life, miracles, and so forth.[21]

The second factor concerns the nature of the incarnate Christ's physical body. His body, which came into existence at a point in time, is, technically speaking, a part of creation. Thus, like all of creation, it is sustained by the threefold operation of the trinity described above.

These two factors together enable us to address the growth and suffering and mortality of the incarnate Christ. In accord with the ontological order, the Father supplied Christ with the power necessary to maintain normal and natural bodily existence. In other words, his physical frame was sustained by a life-force no greater than that allotted any other human being, and therefore he was subject to the same constraints and limitations. His outer-man was bound by natural law and, due to the presence of the sin-principle, susceptible to organic decay and corruption. While his inner-man—or, in his case, divine personality—was not susceptible to organic decay and corruption, it nevertheless received the normal input from his natural senses. Consequently, he felt the usual pain associated with all of his earthly afflictions, including physical trials, aging, and death.[22]

It is significant to note that the Son as Mediator supplied creating and sustaining power to his own body. This accounts for several passages thath allude to the Son's active participation in his own incarnation (Phil. 2:6–7) and his own resurrection (John 2:19; 10:17).

The second question concerns the nature of the incarnate Christ's temptations. Were his temptations real? Could he have actually sinned? At first glance the data appears somewhat confusing. James wrote, "God cannot be tempted by evil" (James 1:13). On the other hand, the New Testament clearly teaches that Jesus was tempted (Matt. 4:1; Mark 1:13; Luke 4:2; Heb. 2:18; 4:15). The biblical evidence provides the theologian with quite a challenge. How does one reconcile the fact that God cannot be tempted with the fact that the Son of God was tempted?

Again, the early church theologians who espoused the two-nature theory provide an answer based on the distinction and the union of Christ's natures. It is assumed that Jesus' divine nature cannot be tempted; consequently, he was tempted in his humanity (i.e., unfallen human nature) alone. Moreover, when his humanity was tempted, it always chose to align with his divinity. "In his condescension God's Son ordinarily chose not to draw on his divine moral strengths, but when in the human nature Jesus judged tempting thoughts to be evil and rejected them, his ethical discernment and action turned out to be in accord with that of the divine nature."[23]

Given that Jesus was susceptible to temptation in his humanity, could he have actually succumbed to temptation and sinned? Assuming that Jesus has two wills, one for each nature, it would seem impossible for him to do so. For in order for Jesus to commit a sin, his human will would need to misalign with his divine will (which could not sin), and such an inner conflict would violate the very nature of the orthodox definition.[24] In short, the incarnate Christ was subject to real temptation in his human nature, but he could not have actually committed a sin due to the presence of his divine nature.

How does the proposed one-nature theory reconcile the fact that God cannot be tempted with the fact that the Son of God was tempted? Before answering this question, a still more basic question needs to be addressed: who is James 1:13 referring to? Who cannot be tempted? It is often assumed that this passage may be applied to any person of the trinity—the Father, the Son, or the Holy Spirit. However, the immediate context of this passage points to a more narrow interpretation. Later in the same chapter, James clearly states that God is "our Father" (1:27, NIV). Since God is called "Father" here, it is reasonable to assume that his earlier reference to God refers to the Father as well. Thus I conclude that James 1:13 applies to the Father alone and says nothing whatsoever about the Son and the Spirit.

Now that the James 1:13 question is out of the way, we may address the original questions: were Christ's temptations real? Could he have actually sinned? I believe that the answer to these questions is *yes*. But before

I state why this is so, a few words about the nature of temptation are in order. Several factors are necessary for true temptation to occur. First, the one tempted must have the power of volition. Volition is the ability to freely choose between alternatives. Second, there must be a set standard to which one is held accountable. From a biblical perspective, God sets the standard of right and wrong. Lastly, one must be tempted to transgress the set standard and do that which should not be done.

In summary, three factors are necessary for true temptation to take place: (1) one must have the power of volition, (2) one must be accountable to a set standard, and (3) one must be tempted to transgress the set standard. I believe that all three factors were met in Christ's temptations. Consider the following.

Did the incarnate Christ have the power of volition? Once again, the ontological order provides valuable insight. In keeping with the ontological order, the Father and the Son relate to one another in a spirit of willing cooperation, mutual respect, and self-giving love. The Father does not demand that the Son do his will, and the Son does not begrudgingly follow the Father's orders. Instead, the Father lovingly directs the Son forward, and the Son chooses to obey the Father's wise counsel. This intimate, loving relationship between the Father and the Son did not change with the incarnation. As they related to one another before this monumental event, they continued to relate to one another after it as well. Thus the incarnate Christ had the power of volition, the freedom to choose between alternatives.

Was the incarnate Christ accountable to a set standard? The Son was not accountable to a set standard before the incarnation, and neither would he be accountable to a set standard after his resurrection. But the incarnate

Christ's time on earth was a unique situation. Jesus was "born of a woman, born under the Law" (Gal. 4:4), and later circumcised according to the Law (Luke 2:21). By coming to earth and identifying with the Jewish people, the Son willfully placed himself under the Mosaic Law. The Law is a works-oriented system, which pronounces blessings for obedience and cursings for disobedience. Furthermore, someone under the Law is obligated to keep all of it (Gal. 3:10; 5:3). Failing in a single point of the Law is the same as breaking the whole Law (James 2:10). Jesus understood his obligation to keep the Law, and he set out to meet the challenge: "Do you think that I came to abolish the Law or the Prophets; I did not come to abolish, but to fulfill" (Matt. 5:17).[25]

Was the incarnate Christ tempted to transgress the set standard? Clearly, Jesus was tempted by the devil to violate the spirit of the Law (Matt. 4:1–11; Mark 1:12–13; Luke 4:1–13). It is also significant to note that someone born tainted by sin—as Jesus was—has an inward bent towards sin, which may be strengthened under the Law. Paul states that the sin-principle uses the Law to its own advantage:

> But sin, taking opportunity through the commandment, produced in me coveting of every kind; for apart from the Law sin is dead. And I was once alive apart from the Law; but when the commandment came, sin became alive, and I died; and this commandment, which was to result in life, proved to result in death for me; for sin, taking opportunity through the commandment, deceived me, and through it killed me (Rom. 7:8–11).

The Law clearly spells out what is right and wrong, and the sin-principle is animated when the conscience is held accountable to such standards. In short, the earth-bound Christ was obligated to keep the Law, and this obligation was challenged from without and from within.

The three factors necessary for true temptation are present in Christ's temptations. During his earthly life, Christ had the power of volition, was accountable to a set standard, and was tempted to transgress the set standard. I conclude, therefore, that the temptations that Jesus faced were real; he could have transgressed the set standard and sinned.

But, also, keep in mind that the Father would not allow Jesus to be tempted beyond what he was able to endure, and he always provided him a way of escape (cf. 1 Cor. 10:13). In each and every case, the incarnate Christ, armed with Holy Scripture and submitting to the Father's guidance given by the Spirit, chose the way of escape. He was "tempted in all things as we are, yet without sin" (Heb. 4:15).

4. *Excursus:* Who Is Omniscient?

"Listen to this, O Job, stand and consider the wonders of God. Do you know how God established them, and makes the lightning of His cloud to shine? Do you know about the layers of the thick clouds, the wonders of one perfect in knowledge" (Job 37:14 16)? It is clear that the God of the Bible is omniscient. He knows all things, including all past, present, and future information. Or, stated a bit differently, God's knowledge is an infinite reservoir of each and every type of information that has been, is, or will be available. This includes, but is not limited to, all information about creation (or both realms) in every category for all time.

Having defined the *what* of God's omniscience, the next question concerns the *who*. Which person of the trinity is omniscient? This may appear to be an unusual question. Since it is typically assumed that omniscience is an attribute of God and that each person of the trinity has all divine attributes, it then follows that each person of the trinity is omniscient. I maintain, however, that there is reasonable evidence to believe otherwise. Earlier I claimed that the Father as Originator is the one true God. Now I propose that Father God alone is omniscient.

Let's start with the words of Jesus concerning the time of his second coming: "But of that day and hour no one knows, not even the angels of heaven, nor the Son, but the Father alone" (Matt. 24:36; cf. Mark 13:32). This statement reveals, either directly or indirectly, something about the knowledge of each person of the trinity. The Father knows when the Son will return; the Son does not know when he will return; and the phrase "the Father alone" indirectly implies that the Spirit does not know when the Son will return. Admittedly, this does not prove that the Father alone is omniscient. It simply states that the Father knows something that the Son and the Spirit do not know. On the other hand, it does narrow down possibilities: the Father knows the "day and hour" and therefore could be omniscient, the Son and the Spirit do not know this and therefore cannot be omniscient.

A case can be made for the Father's omniscience from the New Testament passages that include the word *foreknowledge*. The most revealing example is 1 Peter 1:1–2: "to those who reside as aliens . . . who are chosen according to the foreknowledge of God the Father." Peter's words are doubly significant here because he specifically states that God is the Father and that foreknowledge belongs to him. Also, judging by their immediate context, it is near certain that two other passages credit the Father with foreknowledge. In the book of Acts, Peter declared to the crowd, "this Man [Jesus], delivered up by the predetermined plan and foreknowledge of God [the Father], you nailed to a cross by the hands of godless men and put Him to death" (2:23). In Romans, Paul wrote, "For whom He [the Father] foreknew, He also predestined to become conformed to the image of His Son" (8:29).

Technically speaking, the word "foreknowledge" does not mean omniscience, or all knowing. In these passages it is used primarily to say that God has prior knowledge of something that will take place in time (though some would argue on grammatical grounds that foreknowledge includes purpose as well). On the other hand, it is unlikely that the authors of these passages, well versed in Old Testament Scripture proclaiming God's vast knowledge, would have limited God's foreknowledge to a few isolated things. It is safe to assume that they believed that God's foreknowledge includes any future event, and therefore all future events. In light of the definitions of knowledge and information given earlier, I believe foreknowledge includes, at the very least, all available information about creation for all time—an immense amount of knowledge, which would certainly include details about the Son's return.

It is worth noting that no passage of Scripture ascribes divine foreknowledge to the Son or to the Spirit, and this is in line with the idea that the Father is omniscient and the Son is not. Of course, this is an argument from silence and as such has limited value.

Keep in mind, the idea that the Son and the Spirit lack information does not undermine or diminish their respective person. Invariably, information is something one *has* rather than what one *is*. Each person of the trinity has the capacity to know all things; but actually knowing all things is another matter altogether.

Why is Father God alone omniscient? How can he have intimate foreknowledge of the future yet allow others the privilege of making responsible and meaningful choices in time? Unfortunately, there is not a simple answer to these questions. We have reached the uncomfortable place of enigma and paradox, where mystery and faith rule. While I suspect that the answer is somehow tied in with the Father's place as Originator in the ontological order, addressing such issues here would take us on an arduous detour, to places beyond the charted course of this investigation.

5. Christ's Knowledge

The difficulty in answering the formidable *why* and *how* questions above does not negate what I believe to be a biblically sound position: the Father has all knowledge, while the Son has extensive yet limited knowledge. In regards to the Son's knowledge, the proposed one-nature theory provides a way to determine the types of information he did or did not have access to. The next step is to put this hypothesis to the test. The theological system will now be used to interpret the biblical passages concerning Christ's knowledge given at the beginning of this chapter. Or, in other words, the proposed "unit" will now produce a "product." How well it accomplishes this objective will provide a basis for "quality testing" the system.

What about the passages that show that Jesus had extensive knowledge about many things, including Scripture, the activities of everyday life, all humanity, the nature of sin, the unseen spiritual world, Satan and demons, and historical events? He did not merely have a surface knowledge of these things, but his knowledge was detailed, even to the point of knowing the personal history of an individual. To be sure, Jesus gained a significant amount of information about his immediate environment through his natural senses, and this would account for some of the types of information mentioned here. But, as shown during the course of this investigation, this does not account for all of his past and present information. By the Spirit, Jesus collected all available information in every category from the beginning of creation to the present moment. Certainly, such vast knowledge would include the intimate details of any and all types of historical information.

By extension, the proposed theory also agrees with the Bible on another very important point. The Bible states that, on judgment day, Christ will possess the exacting and comprehensive knowledge necessary to rightly judge all people, the depth of knowledge necessary to "bring to light the things hidden in the darkness and disclose the motives of men's hearts" (1 Cor. 4:5). The proposed theory affirms the same thing in a different way: he will possess all available information from the beginning of creation to the end of the age.

What about the passages that show that Jesus had knowledge about the present? No less detailed is his knowledge of the here and now, such as where to let down the nets to catch fish (Luke 5:4), the location of Nathanael (John 1:48), the motives and thoughts of people, and demonic activity. It is also noteworthy that, as several of these examples show, Jesus did not need to be bodily present to gather this information. Once again, Jesus acquired some of his information through his natural senses. But he gained the majority of it by the Spirit. By the Spirit, Christ acquired all new information in every category as soon as it became available; and, because it was acquired by the Spirit, he did not need to be bodily present to have immediate access to it.[26]

What about the passages that show that Jesus had knowledge about the future? Jesus acquired information about the future in two ways. He acquired it directly from the Father. More than likely, Peter's denials are an example of future information he received in this way. But he also acquired future information from Old Testament Scripture. Biblical prophecy speaks in detail about the Messiah's mission as well as the future state of the world. Jesus understood each prophetic statement in its original context, and he was more than capable of rightly deducing its future application. An example will prove helpful here. Jesus believed that his future passion was the fulfillment of Scripture. He said to his disciples, "Behold, we are going up to Jerusalem, and all things which are written through the prophets about the Son of Man will be accomplished. For He will be delivered to the Gentiles, and will be mocked and mistreated and spit upon, and after they have scourged Him, they will kill Him; and the third day He will rise again" (Luke 18:31–33). In a real sense, Old Testament Scripture was the lens through which Jesus viewed his future as the Suffering Servant.

What about the passages that imply that Jesus lacked knowledge about the future? For example, when he prayed concerning the outcome of future events (Matt. 24:20; Mark 13:18; Luke 22:32). Or, when he stated that he did not know the time of his second coming (Matt. 24:36; Mark 13:32).[27] The proposed one-nature theory is in harmony with the plain meaning of such passages.

Christ had limited access to and incomplete possession of future information.

What about the passages that imply that Jesus lacked knowledge when he asked a question? It is difficult to prove from the prima facie evidence that Jesus lacked knowledge when he asked a question. Significantly, several passages do explicitly state that he asked a question to accomplish a certain objective. In order to test Philip, Jesus asked him where they could buy bread (John 6:5–6). On another occasion, Jesus asked the disciples what they were arguing about (Mark 9:33). However, his immediate response, a lesson on servanthood (vv. 35–37), indicates that he knew their thoughts all along.[28]

Based on the proposed theory, I propose the following solution. Jesus had all past and present information; therefore, he did not ask a question relating to the past or to the present because he needed information, but he did so with purposeful motives in mind. When it comes to questions relating to the future, we have several options. Jesus could have asked those around him a question about the future to test them. Also, since he did not know everything about the future, it is possible that he could have asked someone a question about the future because he needed information.

Naturally, the latter option raises the question, Who would Jesus ask for future information? In short, I believe that Jesus would not have asked his peers for such information, for he knew that their opinion was based on a limited perspective and subject to error. If he could not find the answer in Scripture, he brought the question to his Father in prayer.

What about the passages that claim that Jesus knew "all things" (John 16:30; 21:17)? It must be kept in mind that the disciples who spoke these words heard Jesus say that he did not know something. Therefore, rather than a formal proclamation of divine omniscience, the phrase *all things* should be understood as a contextual response by those who observed Jesus display an extensive amount of knowledge. According to the proposed one-nature theory, "all things" includes intimate knowledge of the other persons of the trinity as well as all information received directly from the Father. It also includes all available information about both realms from the beginning of creation to the present moment. Surely, a Christ with such extensive knowledge would be more than capable of displaying a degree of insight that could bedazzle the disciples and engender such a response.

What about the passages that state that Jesus grew in wisdom (Luke 2:40, 52)? From a biblical perspective, the walk of a wise man is characterized by a consistent and proper application of godly counsel to the circumstances of life. This wisdom-dynamic includes a vertical and horizontal component. A healthy relationship with God provides the vertical means through which one receives divine counsel. The New Testament writers see wisdom as a gift from God. James wrote, "But if any of you lacks wisdom, let him ask God, who gives to all men generously and without reproach, and it will be given to him" (James 1:5). Paul provided even greater clarity. He stated that the Father gives the "spirit of wisdom" (Eph. 1:17), and that the "word of wisdom" is given through the Spirit (1 Cor. 12:8).

Ideally, vertical guidance is followed by the appropriate horizontal application. A truly wise person seeks to apply counsel from *above* to concrete situations *below*. This ongoing struggle to "do the right thing" provides the experiential means for growth, for out of the interactive participation in the wisdom-dynamic flows a personal knowledge of wisdom tested and wisdom vindicated.

This wisdom-dynamic provides the basis for discussing the nature of Christ's wisdom. In keeping with the pattern of the ontological order, the Father, the source of all things, is the fountainhead of wisdom. He imparted wise counsel to the Son by the Spirit (cf. Isa. 11:1–2). The Son then applied the Father's counsel in a consistent and proper manner to each and every circumstance he faced. Thus, by participating in the wisdom-dynamic, Jesus grew in wisdom, a wisdom now known through personal experience.

In summary, this study has revealed the following truths about the incarnate Christ's knowledge. In accord with the ontological order, the Spirit provided the Son immediate access to all present information. But he did not have such access to future information; consequently, he did not know everything about the future. Future information was available to him in one of two ways: either directly from the Father or from Old Testament Scripture. It is not possible to ascertain from the prima facie evidence whether Jesus lacked information when he asked a question. According to the proposed solution, Jesus did not ask "Who touched My garments?" (Mark 5:30), "How many loaves do you have?" (Matt. 15:34), and "Where have you laid him?" (John 11:34) because he lacked knowledge, but he did so with purposeful motives in mind. Similarly, I believe that his questions about the future addressed to his contemporaries were also designed to test them. Jesus only looked heavenward for trustworthy answers about things yet to come.

Life lived with an imperfect knowledge of the future is, to some degree, a life lived by *faith*. Faith "is the assurance of things hoped for, the conviction of things not seen"

(Heb. 11:1). This study concludes that Jesus did, in fact, live by faith; and, as a faithful son who walked the talk, he unconditionally placed himself into His Father's care, both in life and in death.

I contend that the Jesus who increased "in wisdom and stature, and in favor with God and men" (Luke 2:52), "learned obedience from the things which He suffered" (Heb. 5:8), prayed in the garden, "My Father, if it is possible, let this cup pass from Me; yet not as I will, but as Thou wilt" (Matt. 26:39), and said on the cross, "Father, into Thy hands I commit My spirit" (Luke 23:46) is a Son who lived by faith. Is it not comforting to know that our example and advocate faced the future like we do—with some degree of uncertainty? Truly, this Jesus is qualified to teach us how to love and hope and bear suffering, for by faith he has gone through the trials of life and emerged victorious.[29]

6. Christ's Passion

Perhaps the most illuminating discovery of this study was the fact that Christ truly walked by faith. At this time, I would like to provide a practical example from Christ's passion to illustrate this aspect of his life on earth. Christians typically look to the cross as the centerpiece of the faith. It is the place where a holy God and an undeserving sinner find reconciliation. But we often fail to recognize that the cross also provides the supreme expression of faith, i.e., the extraordinary faith displayed by the one nailed to it. By understanding what Jesus experienced on the cross, we gain a tremendous example of faith and self-giving love.

Jesus viewed the cross through the lens of Old Testament Scripture. He saw his destiny as a vicarious sacrifice, a truth foreshadowed in the pages of holy writ. He saw himself as the ram who died in Isaac's place (Gen. 22:9–14), the Passover lamb whose blood was placed on the lintel and doorposts of each home to prevent the destroyer from entering to smite the firstborn (Exod. 12:1–13), the bronze snake lifted up on a pole that provided healing for those fatally wounded (Num. 21:4–9), the Suffering Servant "pierced" for the transgressions of others (Isa. 53:4–6), and the sacrificial animal whose life-blood was poured out at the base of the altar. Certainly, the horror of these word-pictures contributed to Jesus' Gethsemane experience, where he wrestled with the prospect of his forthcoming execution.

There was, however, something more dreadful that awaited him at Calvary. Jesus knew that the following words of the Psalmist would be his: "My God, My God, why hast Thou forsaken Me?" (22:1). The meaning of these words surely haunted him in the garden. The idea of being forsaken by the Father rested upon him like a heavy weight, squeezing out great drops of blood upon his brow. Jesus' greatest joy was to please his Father. But now, ironically, his obedience would incur divine judgment. To accept the cross and thus bear the sins of the whole world meant that he would be subject to the penalty of those sins. Nevertheless, Jesus emerged from the garden willing to drink this "cup," willing to disrupt his intimate relationship with the Father so that others might experience the Father's intimate love.

While reeling on the cross in agony, Jesus did utter the words of the Psalmist (Matt. 27:46; Mark 15:34). At that moment the Father viewed the sinless one as a sinner, a sinner who must suffer the fate of a sinner. For the first and only time, the Son looked up to heaven, beheld a righteous judge, and heard a heart-rending verdict pronounced against him: guilty. The Son was forsaken by the Father; their filial love for one another was disrupted as he received the punishment we rightly deserve.[30] In a manner we will never fully understand, this loss of intimacy caused the Son tremendous anguish and sorrow, a condition that was intensified by the acute pain of crucifixion.

Nevertheless, those moments of anguish on the cross were sustained by an unshakable faith. The same sacred text that foresaw his brutal death gave him hope, for it contained the promise of certain victory. As Jonah was expelled onto dry land after a three-day visit in the belly of a large fish, so Jesus foresaw that his suffering and death was a temporary condition, a temporary condition followed closely by his resurrection and ascension (Matt. 12:40).[31] It is this hope that allowed him to face the unthinkable with a pure faith—a faith to face the future completely abandoned to God, regardless of the present circumstances. Amidst the storm, the Son committed himself into the Father's care: "Father, into Thy hands I commit My spirit" (Luke 23:46). And so the Son of God breathed his last and died, battered and bruised yet not broken, fully believing that victory was just around the corner.

Jesus' faith in the certainty of prophetic utterance was well founded. The New Testament writers clearly state that the Father did, in fact, raise his Son from the dead: "And God [the Father] raised Him [the Son] up again, putting an end to the agony of death, since it was impossible for Him to be held in its power" (Acts 2:24).

It is important to note that the Son's faith in prophetic utterance is ultimately a faith in the Father, the source of prophetic utterance. The Father is omniscient, knowing all past, present, and future information. But the Son did not have such an advantage. He had all past and present information about creation, but he relied on the Father to provide insight into the future. Like us, Jesus lived with a degree of uncertainty as he experienced life on earth, one moment at a time. Without all the details at hand, Jesus had to make authentic, responsible choices, choices that had real consequences and to some extent determined the future. In each and every case, in life and in death, he chose to trust his Father, either his Father's written word (the Old Testament) or his audible counsel.

This raises an interesting question. Assuming that Jesus could have sinned, what would have happened if he actually did? If he chose not to obey his Father? If he transgressed a command of the Law? The answer to this question is truly a sobering one. Jesus the sinner would have suffered grave consequences for his disobedience. He would not have been resurrected from the dead and emerged from the tomb in victory. Instead, he would have remained among the dead, far removed from his heavenly Father's throne and in need of redemption.[32] In addition, Jesus the sinner would have been a blemished "lamb," an unacceptable sacrifice for the sins of others. He could not have provided salvation for the elect in this age and the restoration of the world in the age to come.

If love may be rightly measured by what someone is willing to risk for another, then at the cross the Father and the Son displayed a love for us that is truly a boundless love.

D. Closing Comments

For this study, the manufacturing process of a printing machine provided the pattern for theological development. The manufacturing stages employed thus far in constructing and testing the proposed theological system may be summarized as follows. The process began by fabricating a chassis: a definition of the trinity served as the "chassis," or foundation, of the theological system. Next, components were assembled on the chassis to complete the unit: a theory of the person of Christ was "assembled" on the trinitarian "chassis" to complete the theological system. Finally, the printer produced a product: the complete theological system—or theory of the person of the incarnate Christ established upon a trinitarian foundation—interpreted selected passages relating to the incarnate Christ's knowledge. How well it interprets these passages as well as any associated issues concerning the logical coherence of the system serves as a basis for determining the "quality" of the theological system.

At this point in this investigation, the chassis fabrication, unit assembly, and product production phases have been completed. It is now time to address the quality-testing stage of manufacturing. To this end, I will include an element of comparative analysis, where the orthodox solution will be placed alongside the proposed solution. What does the "quality" of the "product" produced by the orthodox solution say about the "quality" of the orthodox solution? What does the "quality" of the "product" produced by the proposed solution say about the "quality" of the proposed solution? Which solution, if any, passes inspection and is ready to "ship to the customer"? My answer to these questions will complete the last "stage" of this investigation.

According to the orthodox solution, the incarnate Christ is a single person with two natures, one human and the other divine, each nature with its own conscious, will, and attributes. And, as I have discussed earlier, this theory is typically expressed in regard to Christ's knowledge in the following manner: passages that show Christ displaying limited knowledge, such as his ignorance concerning the time of his second coming, are attributed to his human nature, while passages that show him displaying supernatural knowledge, such as his awareness that Peter would deny him in the future, are attributed to his divine nature.[33] As I analyze how this theory interprets each of the selected biblical passages, something catches my eye and raises a red flag. When Jesus was operating within the sphere of his human nature and claimed that he did not know something, what happened to the supernatural knowledge associated with his divine nature? Did he willfully place his divine nature in some sort of subconscious state and therefore cut off his access to this information? How does this affect his deity? When his divine attribute of omniscience is dormant or suppressed, is it reasonable to say that, at those times of inactivity, Jesus is fully God in potentiality but not in actuality? I could continue asking such questions, but I will stop here. Enough has been said to show that the examination of the "product" has exposed something amiss with the system.

Upon further investigation, it is evident that these questions cannot be adequately addressed by making minor adjustments to the system. The issue at hand goes deeper than this. In fact, it goes all the way down to the foundational level. The Nicene Creed states that Jesus is "very God of very God," and the two-nature theory finds an expression for this in his divine nature and his divine attributes. Thus Jesus' deity, his divine nature, and his divine attributes are all tied together. All three stand or fall together. This is clearly seen when it comes to his divine attributes, for to omit or diminish a single attribute is to call into question his full deity.

This logic is seriously challenged when it comes to divine omniscience, perhaps because the claim that Jesus is omniscient is at variance with some clear biblical passages that state that he did not know something (Matt. 24:36; Mark 13:32). Unavoidably, we must choose between one of two options: either we hold that Jesus was omniscient, consciously knowing all things at all times and conflict with the passages that limit his knowledge or we limit his supernatural knowledge in some way to conform to the biblical evidence. In regard to the former case, two fully conscious natures with antithetical attributes operating at one and the same time creates as many problems as it solves. In regard to the latter case, the nagging question of how Jesus can be the embodiment of God and not actively express the sum total or full range of his divine attributes always remains on the horizon. Either way we turn, we are faced with a difficult situation with no easy solution.

We have walked a long road developing the proposed system. Therefore, before discussing the "quality" of this theory, let's first review what it has to say about the person of Christ and how he acquires information.

The incarnate Christ, like all human beings, is a conditional unity of inner-man and outer-man. His outer-man is a real flesh-and-blood body, like that of any other man. His inner-man is a divine personality, which is similar to ours, with basic structural elements in common; yet, at the same time, uniquely set apart and infinitely superior to our personality. While his personality allowed him to experience life as we do, it also enabled him to function in some unique ways: he continued to serve as the Mediator in the ontological order and express the full range of divine faculties (i.e., mind, will, and emotions). Significantly, his natural and supernatural capabilities come into play when we discuss his knowledge.

During his short stay on earth, he acquired information in the following ways: (1) He acquired information about creation through any one of his physical senses, providing him with firsthand knowledge of his physical environment. (2) By the Spirit, who serves as his spiritual "senses," he acquired all present information about creation (or both realms). (3) He acquired future information from one of two sources, the Father or Old Testament Scripture. These three gateways provided Jesus Christ with information—information stored, fully understood, and always at hand.

Having summarized the salient points of the proposed one-nature theory, I will now evaluate the "quality" of the "product" produced by this system. I leave it up to the reader to determine if it is an accurate assessment that hits the center of the target.

The proposed one-nature theory of the incarnate Christ interprets the selected passages relating to his knowledge in a credible manner. Passages that show his extensive knowledge of the past and the present stem from the information he acquired through his natural senses and by the Spirit. Passages that display his knowledge of the future are an expression of the information he acquired from the Father and Old Testament Scripture. And, passages that imply that he lacked knowledge about things to come make sense in light of his limited access to and incomplete possession of future information. Other passages generated questions that focused our attention on some critical issues. What about the passages that imply that Jesus lacked knowledge when he asked a question? What about the passages with the claim that Jesus knew "all things"? What about the passages that state that Jesus grew in wisdom? The proposed theory addresses each question with a reasonable and cogent argument.

The portrait of Jesus that emerges from the pages of this study shows a sage who has comprehensive knowledge of the past and the present, a prophet who has accurate knowledge of the future, a humble servant who, with limited knowledge, walks by faith, and a king who will possess all the knowledge necessary to serve as judge at the end of the age.[34]

After quality inspecting the "product" of each system, I have arrived at the following conclusion. Both theological systems provide a possible way to interpret the selected passages relating to Christ's knowledge. However, while interpreting these passages, the orthodox solution was found to have a "flaw" in the system proper, a difficulty that requires substantial rework of some kind. Conversely, the proposed solution interpreted the same passages without exposing an inherent problem with the system, either at the foundational level or with the system as a whole. Thus the "product" of the proposed system testifies to a smooth-running "unit," which is ready for "delivery."

Notes

1. Jesus also spoke of himself as a man (John 8:40).
2. W. E. Elwell, ed., *Evangelical Dictionary of Theology*, p. 204.
3. P. Schaff, *The Creeds of Christendom,* vol. 2, p. 62.
4. Ibid.

5. The idea that Christ had one will, called monothelitism, was officially condemned at the Third Council of Constantinople in 680.
6. A. F. Johnson and R. E. Webber, *What Christians Believe* (Grand Rapids: Zondervan Publishing House, 1989), p. 134.
7. L. Berkhof, *Systematic Theology,* p. 321.
8. Several suggested readings are T. C. Oden, *Systematic Theology,* vol. 2: *The Word of Life* (New York: HarperCollins, 1989), pp. 164–194, and G. R. Lewis and B. A. Demarest, *Integrative Theology,* vol. 2 (Grand Rapids: Zondervan Publishing House, 1990), pp. 309–367. For a contemporary incarnational Christology, see M. J. Erickson, *The Word Became Flesh* (Grand Rapids: Baker Book House, 1991), pp. 507–576.
9. For an excellent summary of the Word-flesh Christologies of Athanasius and Apollinarius, as well as the orthodox reaction to the latter, see J. N. D. Kelly, *Early Christian Doctrines* (New York: HarperCollins, 1978), pp. 284–301.
10. M. J. Erickson, *The Word Became Flesh,* p. 61.
11. For more details see J. L. Gonzalez, *A History of Christian Thought,* vol. 1 (Nashville: Abingdon Press, 1987), pp. 349–352.
12. M. J. Erickson, *Christian Theology* (Grand Rapids: Baker Book House, 1985), p. 536.
13. Ibid., p. 536–7.
14. Ibid., p. 537.
15. Significantly, the New Testament writers describe Jesus' inner man as a spirit (John 11:33; 13:21; 19:30) and a soul (12:27).
16. The idea that Jesus was born in sin is not completely foreign to Christianity. For example, "Reinhold Nieber and Carl Barth hold that since Jesus was tempted in all points as we are, He must have had a sinful nature like our fallen nature" (G. R. Lewis and B. A. Demarest, *Integrative Theology,* vol 2 [Grand Rapids: Zondervan Publishing House, 1990], p. 336).
17. While this is true, that this "tainting" is not a person, it is difficult to describe what it does in non-personal terms. Perhaps this is so because it is so closely associated with human personality that the two tend to blend together and appear as one. Nevertheless, throughout the following discussion, it is important to remember that, when describing it the use of personal language does not imply the existence of a personality.
18. The phrase *because all sinned* is very difficult to interpret. Is Paul implying that in some collective sense all humanity was in Adam when he sinned (cf. Heb. 7:9–10), and thus all humanity sinned with him? If so, does this mean that each individual inherits both sin *and* guilt at birth? These are controversial questions, which are difficult to answer on the basis of this passage

alone. Personally, I do not believe that this phrase should be interpreted in such a way to negate personal responsibility. In other words, I believe that people are born in sin (with the sin-principle present and active within) but not born guilty sinners. The latter is a condition which hinges on willful choice.
19. The idea that Jesus was born tainted by sin does not demean Mary. Neither does it make woman the sole propagator of sin. I question the notion that sin is passed down from generation to generation like physical traits. Jesus did not inherit the sin-principle through a process of parent-to-child infusion, but he became sin-infected simply by entering into and becoming part of an already sin-infected creation.
20. T. C. Oden, *The Word of Life,* p. 185.
21. See subsection titled Divine References for passages on creative acts and sustaining life. Concerning miracles, the flow of power is seen in Acts 10:38: "You know of Jesus of Nazareth, how God [the Father] anointed Him with the Holy Spirit and with power, and how He went about doing good, and healing all who were oppressed by the devil; for God was with Him" (cf. 2:22).
22. Jesus suffered fatigue during his ministry, and therefore he needed rest to rejuvenate himself. Scripture records one occasion when he was sleeping in the stern of a boat (Matt. 8:24; Mark 4:38). In general, sleep is "a suspension of voluntary bodily functions and the natural suspension, complete or partial, of consciousness" (*Random House Webster's College Dictionary*). In Jesus' case sleep was somewhat different due to his unique personality. His mode of rest included the cessation of voluntary bodily functions; however, he was sufficiently conscious during these times to continue to perform his role in the ontological order.
23. G. R. Lewis and B. A. Demarest, *Integrative Theology,* vol. 2, p. 344.
24. An inner conflict of this kind results in some form of Nestorianism. Nestorianism was rejected by the Synod of Ephesus in A.D. 431.
25. I am focusing here on Jesus' obligation to keep the Law, not when in his life he became accountable to keep it. The *when* question is difficult to answer, especially in light of his uniqueness. The proposed theory maintains that Jesus was not an ordinary child. His inner-man was fully conscious at all times, exercising the full perfection of divine personality at each stage of physical development. Moreover, as Mediator of the Law, he did not have to learn it, for he had a complete knowledge of it from his first breath to his last. Moral consciousness and knowledge of this nature as-

sumes accountability. All things considered, I am uncomfortable giving a definite age of accountability. Nevertheless, several things seem reasonable to assume. Jesus was only accountable for those aspects of the Law which were incumbent upon (1) whatever age he happened to be at a given time and (2) his particular status within the community (For example, he was not married or a temple priest.).

26. On the surface, the fig tree incident recorded by Mark (11:12–14) appears to conflict with what I am saying here. A quick look at the pertinent verse will show that things are not as simple as this: "And seeing at a distance a fig tree in leaf, He [Jesus] went to see if perhaps He would find anything on it; and when he came to it, He found nothing but leaves, for it was not the season for figs" (v. 13).

    When viewed as a whole, this verse is somewhat confusing. Mark says that Jesus checked the fig tree for fruit at a time of the year when fig trees do not produce fruit! It is possible that Jesus did not know the condition of the tree, and he checked it for fruit despite the fact that it was not fruit-bearing season. But it is just as likely, if not more so, that Jesus knew it was not fruit-bearing season and he did not expect to find fruit on the tree, but he went ahead and checked it for fruit anyway, simply to add a dramatic visual component to his parable.

    Obviously, the latter interpretation is consistent with the proposed theory, where the Spirit would have provided Jesus with the true condition of the fig tree before he went up to it and checked it for fruit.

27. Jesus expressed amazement in response to faith (Matt. 8:10; Luke 7:9) or the lack of faith (Mark 6:6). The idea that Jesus did not have all future information provides for a natural context for his behavior.

28. Several other Gospels record this incident in a different manner. Matthew says that the disciples asked Jesus who is the greatest in the kingdom of heaven (18:1–5). Luke simply states that Jesus knew their thoughts (9:4648). More than likely, the Gospel writers are recording the same incident highlighting different details. D. A. Carson writes, "It is not difficult or unnatural to suppose that Jesus detected their rivalry (Luke), challenged them, and thereby silenced them (Mark), and that they then blurted out their question (Matthew)" (*The Expositor's Bible Commentary,* vol. 8 [Grand Rapids: Zondervan Publishing House, 1984], p. 396). Despite the difficulty harmonizing these accounts, my point still stands. Jesus did not ask the question in

Mark's account because he needed information, for he knew their thoughts all along.
29. In this study, I focused on Jesus as he walked this earth, and defined him accordingly. As discussed above, the result was a Christ of faith. I also believe that this same Jesus who lived by faith *then* lives by faith *now*. This position brings Jesus' current role as intercessor to life, making it more believable, relatable, and filled with passion.
30. This "disruption" did not suspend all functional aspects of the ontological order, otherwise creation would cease to exist. The Father and the Son continued to relate to one another but, in a real sense, as business partners rather than loving kin.
31. Jesus could have found evidence for his own resurrection and ascension in the Old Testament. His resurrection is inferred in passages such as Psalm 16:9–10 and Hosea 6:1–2, and his ascension in, for example, Psalm 68:18. Surely, he also saw such events in passages that proclaim his future exaltation (see Ps. 2:8–9).
32. Remember, Jesus would not be in "torment" here, but in "comfort" with Abraham and the other Old Testament saints (see Luke 16:19–31). In this mode of existence, he could maintain his place and function in the ontological order.
33. For more examples, see section titled Two-Nature Theory.
34. Can we take things a step further and refine what has been said about Jesus' knowledge? Can we be more specific on what he did or did not know? What about Jesus' current knowledge? Can we be more specific about what he does or does not know today? Such questions are legitimate. But there are limits as to how far we can go. The Bible provides us our only reliable source of data, and it is very selective. Inevitably, the quest for greater precision leads to greater speculation. In order to limit unnecessary speculation, I have attempted to conduct this investigation under controlled conditions, using a selective group of passages to evaluate the proposed solution. Admittedly, this approach leaves questions unanswered. In the future, perhaps some hard work and creative input will help to refine things. Until then, I hope that unanswered questions do not distract—or possibly prevent—the reader from wrestling with the main thrust of the proposed argument.

Appendix: Comparison Table

	Orthodox Solution	**Proposed Solution**
God	A Trinity of Father, Son, and Holy Spirit	The Father as the source of all things, the fountain of life and wisdom, and the chief architect who oversees everything that takes place in creation.
Trinity	Three persons of one substance/essence.	The Father, Son, and Holy Spirit in a fixed and eternal arrangement which governs their relationship with one another and with creation.
Attributes of God	The characteristics or qualities which define God as God. Each person of the trinity has all divine attributes.	A "divine attribute" is a truth about a person or the persons of the trinity.
Omnipresence	Each person of the trinity is omnipresent; though Christ was located in a body while on earth.	The Father and the Son are in heaven (except for the Son's brief stay on earth), while the Holy Spirit fills heaven and earth.
Omnipotence	Each person of the trinity is omnipotent; though Christ may be empowered by the Spirit.	The Father is the source of all power, and he exercises his power through the Son and by the Spirit.

	Orthodox Solution	**Proposed Solution**
Omniscience	Each person of the trinity is omniscient; though Christ lacked knowledge in his human nature.	The Father is omniscient, while the Son has vast yet limited knowledge.
Person of Christ	Christ has two natures, one human and the other divine, each nature with its own conscience, will, and attributes.	Christ has one nature, encompassing a "divine" personality, which is similar yet uniquely set apart and infinitely superior to human personality.
Deity of Christ	Christ is "very God of very God, begotten, not made, being of one substance with the Father."	The identification of Christ as God is an expression of the revelation of God in Christ.
Christ's "Sinfulness"	Christ on earth was untainted by sin, like Adam before the Fall.	Christ on earth was tainted by sin, like all human beings since the Fall.
Christ's Temptations	Christ suffered real temptation in his human nature, but he could not sin due to the presence of his divine nature.	Christ's temptations were real; he could have sinned but chose not to.
Work of Christ	The Son united with complete humanity (a human nature and a physical body) to save complete humanity.	The Son fully identified with humanity and thus served as an acceptable substitute for humanity.
Worship	The triune God is the object of worship; and each person of the trinity may be worshiped as God.	The one true God, the Father is worshiped through the Son and by the Spirit.